TRASH TO CASH

The Step-By-Step Guide to Building a Profitable Media Business.

Hayden Aquilon

Dedication

I want to thank my amazing wife Alexandria for everything she has made possible for our family.

There is no possible way I could have ever built our business or created this book without you.

It's amazing how far we have come in just two short years since we started our business. I can't wait to see where it leads us. I'll bet it's beyond our wildest dreams. There is nothing we can't accomplish together.

I love you to the moon & back.

Table of Contents

$ Selling Books Direct to Consumer Sites
$ Wholesaling
$ Selling to Buyback Sites
$ When Is It Time to Hire?
$ Scaling up
$ Micro Goals
$ Take Immediate Action
$ Find Accountability Partners Doing the Same Thing

$ Mindset
$ Hardware
$ Software
$ Bookmark Tab
$ Importance of Networking
$ Influencers to Follow
$ Trust...But Verify

$ Cost Per Book
$Average Sale Price
$ Average Payout Per Book
$ Sell Through Rate
$ Cost Per Lead
$ Tracking Key Performance Indicators (KPI's)
$ Cash Flow vs. Your Burn Rate
$ Ebbs and Flows

$ Time for A Rant!
$ Playing the Long Game

PART ONE: HEAR ME OUT

Leading up to it all

At some point, you were probably asked several times what you wanted to be when you grew up. I can certainly recall several different occasions when I was asked by my mom, and my response was always the same, "I want to be a millionaire".

Now, I am not sure I actually knew what being a millionaire sincerely meant at the time, but I do know why I desired it.

I knew millionaires were "rich" and did not have to worry about money (or so I thought). Deep down it wasn't that I wanted to be rich, surrounded by nothing but lavish things. All I wanted was to not worry about where our next meal was coming from.

There were many years when times were tough and emotions ran high at my mom's house over money, food, and bills.

I will be the first to admit that we certainly weren't homeless or starving, but things seemed pretty grim at times.

From that point in my life, it is clear to me now, that I developed a negative belief system about money. It occurred to me that money was something that was hard to get and even harder to keep while not abundant at all. If anything, it was extremely scarce.

My parents had been divorced since I was six, and my mom struggled to put food on the table intermittently throughout my childhood. Our family was constantly living out of fear because of money, and it affected everything.

Being a single mom with three young kids makes it tough to go out and get a job. Luckily, we all got through the tough times together.

What certainly didn't help the overall situation was where I was born and raised. I grew up in the small town of Santa Barbara, CA where famous people such as Oprah Winfrey, Kathy Ireland, and Kevin Costner reside.

It is the best place on earth. You are surrounded by nothing but sand, ocean, and mountains while living in perfect weather year-round.

If you have ever been fortunate enough to live there, or even visit, you will know what I mean.

It's the kind of town where 16-year old's parents buy them a BMW or a Range Rover for their birthday.
Some parents are founders of companies you have heard of, actors, attorneys, and most are good old trust fund babies.

I remember constantly thinking to myself, "If money is so scarce and hard to get, then why does there seem to be so much abundance everywhere I turn? How can I make that kind of money?"

In hindsight, I now realize that being surrounded by that kind of wealth on a constant basis not only motivated me to my core, but it also normalized that lifestyle for me.

It set up a high bar for me. I swore to myself that I would do anything it took to get to that level of financial success.

It didn't matter what kind of roadblocks were in my way, I was determined to go over, under, or straight through anything in my path.

The Good Ol' Trap

Fast forward a handful of years to College. I still hadn't figured out the secret to financial success and continued to chase the quick buck. Apparently, I didn't want to put in the hard work and patience to achieve this personal desire for success.

How can you blame an ambitious young man growing up in an environment like Santa Barbara?

Since moving out on my own at age 18, with bills already piling up and rent to pay, the sensible thing to do would have been to take a job in the industry I was most fond of – finance.

A paid internship in accounting would have been ideal to get my foot in the door. But, let's face it, I was young and impatient.

So, what did I end up doing? I took the easy road, of course, bussing tables at a well-known restaurant. The tips were incredible, and I could easily walk away making $150-$160 in tips a night + wages.

Through hard work I quickly advanced to become a bartender there and started making even more in tips.

During this time, I was enrolled in Santa Barbara City College taking my education seriously (okay, half-ass at best).

This particular bartending job was extremely well paying to the point where several older gentlemen have made this their career.

What that job allowed me to do was keep up with well-to-do friends, party on a consistent basis, and travel wherever I wanted to go.

Meanwhile, I was seriously eroding my long-term chance at success without even realizing it.

I was the guy at the bar who knew everyone, always loving to buy the shots and getting bottle service at the clubs with my buddies.

There were several times when I thought to myself that this could be enough. I mean what more do I need? I had plenty of money to live comfortably. No priorities. No worries. The service industry was amazing!

In reality, it was all a huge trap. It is what one would call a slow death.

In addition to killing myself working double shifts six days a week, and drinking enough to kill a small horse, it lacked any aspect of continuous learning, excitement, and self-fulfillment.

Please don't misunderstand me - I am not saying that working in the service industry is not an honorable or fulfilling profession. Many hardworking individuals take pride in it and make an honest living. For me, I just needed more. Plain and simple.

Eventually, seeing the dire reality of my situation, I started to understand how short-sided I was in my thinking and my actions. I didn't like the direction I was heading in and my future looked quite grim.

I knew it was time for a change.

As the gradual shift started to happen, it wasn't as simple as waking up one day and making huge sudden changes in my everyday life. I didn't have some life altering moment like many guru's eventually tout.

I didn't have a near death experience or wake up as a changed man. No, it happened subtly...so subtly one could almost dismiss its occurrence altogether.

In hindsight, what it all boils down to is choosing that you want - no, that you NEED, a significant change. If you aren't bought in, you're going to fail fast.

You've probably heard this uttered several times before at some point in your life, but here is the difference.

<u>You don't have to try and convince yourself you're fed up; you ARE fed up</u>. And because you are fed up, you take massive action to change your circumstances.

The truth is, I didn't NEED it bad enough, I simply wanted it…. success sounded nice. If you were ever around me, I sounded like a broken record making statements like:

"Man, I wish I were rich right now, I'm tired of waiting."
"I wish I had that car, I deserve it."
"Wow, it must be nice to have a house like that."
"It's so unfair I didn't come from money."

What a whiny entitled kid I was.

The problem with America today is that we've been conditioned to want things now, and we don't want to wait for it.

These days, you tend to hear that millennials are the worst at working towards something.

I can agree with that, but only up to a certain point. Hear me out on this! It's not that millennials are somehow lazy pieces of poop – they are simply a product of the current environment.

Think about it, depending on what past generation you were born into, your options of work were severely limited, and most people were just happy to have a steady source of income.

It didn't matter what you had to do or how long you had to do it, you were ready to sacrifice for your family (think Industrial Revolution, WWI & WWII).

People were in survival mode.

Why do you think that most baby boomers are so frugal and hardworking? They have honor, respect, and manners. They look up to their elders. This isn't a coincidence, they are a product of their environment.

Things are completely different now. Millennials are smart (of course there are plenty of dumb ones too). They have tons of options open to them. They have instant access to education and self-help that all previous generations did not have at their fingertips (think Google, Podcasts, and YouTube). What people like Tim Ferriss call "lifestyle design" is big now.

You no longer have to work to survive in harsh times. Opportunities are endless and there is work everywhere. As I write this, unemployment is incredibly low.

How can you blame them for wanting to be nomadic, or not working long, 15-hour days? Sometimes it's even hard to blame them for living paycheck to paycheck.

Let's not forget about the good old information overload. We have come to a time in life where you are getting beaten over the head by content.

Email auto-responders, commercials, ads, automated phone calls from a Chinese person trying to sell you something in a foreign language (WTF???).

Meanwhile companies and individuals have taken the liberty to capitalize on this shift in thinking – and rightly so.

You're fat – here, take this pill for a quick fix. Buy this course and you'll make millions in two days from now. Use our credit card to splurge with your friends. Buy now, pay later!

The overlying message: Don't deprive yourself of the life you desire – YOU DESERVE IT NOW!!!!.

We have ALL been guilty of getting sucked into this at one point or another (Let's face it, platforms like Instagram haven't helped, but they are not totally to blame).

And that's not the crazy part. The crazy comes from people who keep buying into the same trap! Flocks of people continuously buying one thing after another to fix the same problem.

When I eventually got the courage to move out of state from my beautiful hometown, I choose Austin, TX to make my new home.

At this point, I knew I had to get serious if I wanted to become financially successful. I had formulated what I thought was a good plan of action that I was going to follow religiously. I didn't care how long it would take – I was determined to make it a reality.

Soul-Sucking 9-5's

"Hello, my name is Hayden and I hate my job". That was me for years. The 9-5 drudgery is harsh. I could have gone to AA meetings, but for the workplace instead.

I will never forget one of my top 5 reads called "unscripted" by one of my favorite authors - MJ Demarco.

His description of his 9-5 commuting experience hit me so deep and emotional, that I found myself crying and laughing hysterically. His message? Working like that is so depressing, and he's absolutely right.

Read this passage from his book and tell me you can't identify:

"F@%k. It's Monday morning, 5:15 a.m. For the third time, my iPhone is screaming that Nickelback song I once loved, but now hate. Another snooze and I'll be late.

Yes, it's time to wake up. I yank myself out of bed, slightly hungover from the night before. I dread the day – actually no, the week-to come. Needing a jump start, I stumble into the shower, hoping for a clean perspective. No luck.

The forthcoming day rivals getting a colonoscopy. As I lynch-tie my neck and arm my suit, regret and resignation ravage my soul. Something is not right.

Perhaps it's the $800 suit. Perhaps it's the credit card that paid for the suit. Perhaps it's the stinking realization that my weekend highlight was watching two mediocre football teams play in the Las Vegas Bowl.

Perhaps it's the morning darkness and the stark reality that my short Cancun vacation is still months away. Unfortunately, this is no time for a Jesus moment.

With moments to eat, I grab an artificially colored bowl of sugar-coated grain. With one eye on the clock and another on the meal plan pinned to the refrigerator – the one I'm supposed to follow religiously for the next eight weeks – I blame Toucan Sam for my first transgression."

LOL - So, was I right?

Are you reading this on your iPhone while camping out on the toilet at work? Do you dream of walking into your boss' office and quitting every day? (with the exception of Friday at 4:59pm).

Are you finding yourself faking sick on Fridays or Mondays just to get through the week? How about happy hours during the week to get by, only to feel hungover as heck the next morning?

Aren't you getting sick and tired of that routine week in and week out? I am telling you it doesn't have to be like that!

You need to be real with yourself, don't try and sugar coat things. If you feel like your situation is terrible, then it IS terrible. Stop whining and feeling sorry for yourself and figure out a plan.

Stop delaying and telling yourself you're just lucky to have a job. There are endless opportunities out there right now.

Not just for a different job (that you may actually enjoy more), but to create a lifestyle that you can specifically design for yourself and enjoy (Hence a lifestyle entrepreneur).
 By the way, if you support a family with little savings and low income, I would hope you have enough sense to do what is necessary to take care of your family.

I hear some guys who leverage their house, max out their credit cards, and put a title loan on their car to chase their childhood dream of inventing some stupid product no one wants.

You should never have to put yourself in that situation. If you find yourself headed down that path you should stop and take a good look at yourself in the mirror.

I have realized over the years that you really can validate anything through a "side hustle" and grow it from there. Worst case scenario is that it doesn't work as planned and you are back to the drawing board, BUT you still have your job and your family is taken care of.

My clear and concise goal for this book is to show you the path I have taken through Amazon and how it has opened endless doors for me. It can certainly do the same for you. I'm telling you it will, but only if you let it. You need to give this opportunity a chance.

There is so much money to be made around Amazon it blows my mind. Trust me when I say that no matter what your situation, there is a path that fits your time and financial constraints.

We all have such a tremendous opportunity to make money on Amazon, and it is completely unrivaled by any other platform online at this time.

This is the wild part - Amazon is just getting started with their many opportunities that they offer.

If you haven't caught on to the obvious realization of what Amazon is, they are basically what Google is to online search, but for shopping online.

We are beginning to see this already, but in the near future websites for products will become completely prehistoric and obsolete. The entire shopping experience will be taking place on platforms like Amazon.

Companies must go to where their customers are already shopping and the stats are in - over 50% of all online sales occurred on Amazon this past year (2019)!!

It is much more expensive for a company to try and pay for advertising to lead customers away from where they're already looking. Why try and lead them elsewhere to make a sale?

This is especially true if where they are shopping is Amazon. Making a move like that is almost guaranteed to be a less cost-effective use of marketing dollars in the short-term.

Sure, one day you will want to take orders off of Amazon on your own platform and collect your own customer data. This will come at a later time.
Regardless of what platform you sell on, you can still have the freedom and control over how much you make. I am going to give you everything you need to succeed in this book.

This isn't your average book. I'm not some guy that built a multi-billion-dollar business and I'm going to tell you about how I did it all 20 years ago. What is interesting to me is how people think that someone like that is the absolute authority on ALL business building.

Let me explain. First of all, if you are truly looking to build a billion-dollar business – good luck to you on that one. I can only take you so far into your journey.

If you want to design a life of financial freedom you don't need to build anything close to that.

You see, it takes a whole different mindset and playbook for building something that large.

Creating a small business that does $250,000-$1,000,000/year for example, is an entirely different playbook.
You approach it much differently. I happen to have that experience in building up a lifestyle business to that level and the best part is, I didn't do it 20 years ago. I did this recently (and still operating it, by the way).

I believe if you don't have a goal/plan of where you want to take this kind of business (or any business in general) you need to immediately sit down and map that out.

If you don't know what your destination is, how can you expect to get there??
Come join me and let me show you all the ways you can achieve this. I'm going to show you the exact route that I took and show you how to formulate a plan on how to get to the numbers you are aiming for!

PART TWO: WHAT ARE YOUR OPTIONS?

Words of Caution

Almost certainly over the last couple years you've seen hundreds, if not thousands of advertisements from people trying to sell you online courses on Amazon for private labeling products.

Most of these individuals have been trying to capitalize on a big misconception that has been going on where you can make millions of dollars overnight on platforms like Amazon.

"Go on Alibaba, find a cool product, throw it up on Amazon and WHAAALAA!!! YOU'RE RICH!"

These misconceptions were turned into a huge opportunity for shady marketers and a maxed-out credit card for shiny object chasers.

Right now, at the time of this writing, Amazon is the current HOT thing. And like anything that is considered "the next best thing," there is a limited shelf-life to it (the hype that is, not Amazon as a platform).

This typically happens in the shape of a bell curve. The bell curve starts off with a slow rise as word spreads of the opportunity.

It then begins to hockey stick up to the right exponentially as people are finding these new opportunities and going all-in (either from heightened word of mouth, advertising, or celebrity endorsements).

Where you start to see a slowdown is when the current landscape becomes oversaturated with shiny object chasers, and it is found that the opportunity was grossly misrepresented and hyped up (especially in this case).

This is when you see the bell curve start to flatten out at the top and then take a nosedive back down the other side.

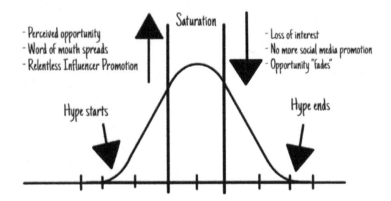

Let me be the one clear voice of reason and tell you that misconceptions like these are akin to the plague - avoid them at all costs!

All those guys pushing multi-million-dollar businesses in the first-year non-sense are turds. I have been a consultant on Amazon since 2015, helping over a dozen clients - many of which were running successful companies both in Amazon and outside of Amazon.

Even the most successful ones barely topped the $1,000,000 in sales mark on Amazon alone (after already having a following and being on Amazon for a few years).

Many of these brands are established, have email lists, and are stocked on retailer's shelves.

"But Hayden, I've seen the guru's screenshots of their sales" LOL, guess what – even if some of these guru's screen shots were actually real and showed a company getting to that million-dollar level, I'll bet you that doesn't mean jack.

Why? It's SALES. WHO CARES. What's your profit on all that? I know companies that boast $1,000,000 in sales and spend $1,500,000 in ad spend to get it LOL. Do you see the problem here??

Ever wonder why they don't show a profit and loss statement or a screenshot of their QuickBooks overview? Lol.

Private Label Pitfalls

I owned my own brand where I did private label for two years in the health and fitness arena. I had access to many resources that most newcomers do not - A great group of advanced sellers, mentors, and good finances.

The largest month I ever had was $17,000 in sales. Sales...not profits. And no, I wasn't able to live off that.

What ultimately happened was that I underestimated the very competitive market I was in. I started off great and had a healthy profit margin. Unfortunately, I did not accurately assess my competition, fulfillment costs, cost of goods, and retail prices that continued to be lowered by price wars with direct competitors.

On top of that, Chinese manufacturers started to get a piece of the action as well. As you can very well guess, they have a major advantage due to rock bottom cost of goods.

This is not a unique situation. This is a major issue facing many Amazon sellers. Everyone is taught the same thing.

Go out and find a similar product on Alibaba.com and tweak it a tad. Then just buy it and throw it up on Amazon and you're good!

Think about this - what have they done to make a unique product? 99% of the time absolutely nothing. They just copied a listing they noticed on Amazon or Alibaba. Where is the value you are bringing to the marketplace?

This particular person is going to get beaten down by competition and have to spend a fortune to outspend others on things like ads, reviews, and brand influencers just to be seen!

On Amazon, you have to rank for keywords to actually appear anywhere near the top of the search results. To rank for certain keywords, you need SALES. And guess what, you don't get sales until you are SEEN. Get it?

Private label is expensive, despite what others say. Yes, you do need to have tens of thousands of dollars to start a private label brand. Especially if that brand does well and you need to scale up.

If you do have a successful launch, you will quickly find that you will be having to put down tens of thousands of dollars to get larger and larger shipments. On one of my last shipments for my private label company I spent $20,000 on one SKU for a single order.

Don't fall into the trap of thinking you can start private label for cheap - you simply can't. If you're maxing out credit cards you are making a big mistake, one that is very risky and could be costly down the road.

Simply put - you are a fool if you try to start private label from a bad financial standpoint.

In case you are wondering if you are an ideal candidate to try your hand in private label, let me illustrate my point here. Let me give you an example of someone who is perfect to start a private label business and someone who should have no business starting a private label company.

Let's start with the one who should <u>not</u> be doing this type of business. John is 50 years old and has three children ages 8 to 20 years old. His yearly income is 55,000 and his wife is a part-time teacher's aide. Let's say the combined incomes are 75,000 per year.

They currently have a mortgage and are financing both their cars and their kid's education. At the end of the month, they hardly ever have anything left over and hold a regular credit card account balance of $8000, which they can't pay off and are stuck paying the minimums.

This, my friends, is disastrous for someone who's thinking they want to do private label - please do not try to do that at this stage.

That's not to say that this couple will never be able to do private label in the future. What I would try and do in their situation is wait until the kids get older and their financial situation improves.

On the other hand, we have Jim. Jim is a 32-year-old sales rep at a large company that has a long-standing track record of growth and profits. In other words, he's with a reliable company that's not going to go under at any moment.

Jim does not have any student loan debt or credit card debt. He currently rents an apartment that costs him $1000 per month. He owns his own car out right. It's a used car, but it's a good car that he bought back when he was in college.

In a bad year Jim brings home $95,000. In a good year, he can make as much is $180,000. He also has been maxing out his 401(k) and his savings account is sitting at $60,000 in cash. This is the type of person who has every opportunity and advantage to start a private label business.

Hopefully many of you are not in John's situation. Many of you may be younger and without kids, but you may not be in good financial standing.

Unfortunately, many of you are riddled with credit card debt and student loans. That is not an ideal starting point for private label.

If I had to guess, I would say less than 5% of people make it building a successful private label business. That means that you have a better chance of walking into a casino with all your dough and putting it on red or black at a roulette table.

Are you beginning to see the difference here? You are asking for disaster if you combine a high-risk venture with a high-risk type of financial situation.

You need to truthfully look at your situation and ask yourself if you're in a position to take on a private label business or is there a better route, such as retail arbitrage?

In most cases, I'll bet it is retail arbitrage. That is the argument that I want to make to you in this book. After all, it is the smarter play.

Retail arbitrage is simple. You buy and sell other people's goods. It's cost effective, there is no advertising involved, and you don't need to invent anything.
Somewhat recently, there was yet another major setback for many private label sellers. A substantial increase in tariffs on

goods that were being imported from China. Up to a 25% increase! For many people that obliterated their margins entirely.

Talk about a volatile playing field.

Don't look at this and think, "No, it will be different for me." I can guarantee you with 99% certainty it will not be. You are not immune to this!

*I am not saying private label is impossible to do, what I am saying is the odds are EXTREMELY stacked against you. There are so many factors in play.

At this point in the book, I strongly urge you to get out a pen to highlight, and some sticky notes.

Not only will you retain information better if you mark up the book, but I want you to really make an effort to notate your action plan and steps. I will be outlining them in the coming chapters and it would be wise for you to ACTUALLY use this book you bought to make you money.

Hang in there and let me tell you about a much safer & cost-effective way to sell on Amazon.

One that WHEN you succeed at this (not IF), you can make the choice to move over to doing your own private label business in a much better position of knowledge and experience.

In addition, you can use the foundation and cashflow from retail arbitrage to fund your future venture in private label – should you choose to.

Now, had I not ultimately failed at my first attempt at a private label business and decided right then and there that Amazon business are impossible (like so many do), I would have missed out on so many great opportunities that followed.

At this point in my Amazon journey, I now have 3 different revenue streams and I am working on my 4th at the time of this writing.

The point I'm trying to make is that there IS money to be made on Amazon, but if you're one of those people that is constantly jumping ship, and looking for the next best thing - you're toast. Amazon is a <u>LONG</u> game.

You need to eliminate that mindset completely. On and off Amazon you have to be absolutely focused on one venture at a time. It is imperative for your success.

You are not going to make a million dollars right off the bat – or ever, for that matter, but you absolutely can make a decent living doing something you love.

When I had "failed" at private label that wasn't actually a loss at all for me. Even at the time I knew it.

I quickly realized my mistakes and reasoned I had better go back to the drawing board and look at some different business models.

What I realized is that if you can entrench yourself in the various income streams that Amazon has, and do it early enough, you are going to have a significant leg up over other individuals that decide to jump in and get their piece of the pie down the road.

Since Amazon has been around for many years, you may be thinking you are too late to the game and there is no point in starting. Let me tell you - that is simply not true.

There are still endless opportunities for you to either start your own brand, do retail arbitrage, become a consultant for other companies, wholesale other people's products, design your own clothing wear, create ebooks, etc.

Heck, at the time of this writing, Amazon is looking for people who want to start their own driving/delivery business that delivers Amazon products and they are willing to make loans to anyone that will do this.

They boast that you can make up to $300,000 a year with your own fleet.

I don't care how smart you are, what your income level is, what your talents are, or where you grew up - there is an opportunity for anyone out there to make an impact on their life. You have so many choices available to you, it is unreal. Are you getting excited yet?

It is there for the taking. I am personally not aiming to build a billion-dollar business. I don't want a bunch of employees whose names I don't know, nor do I want shareholders.

I'm looking to build a lean and mean 7-8 figure business with other "passive" income streams that generate enough money to live the lifestyle that I want.

If I'm fortunate enough to reach revenue levels I've never dreamed of, then so be it. Bring it on.

No matter what your ambitions are, I can guarantee you that Amazon can either support it or be the launch pad to get you where you want to be.

There are people that are going to read this and say, "having an Amazon business isn't a real business because you don't own the channel. Amazon can ban you immediately if they want, blah blah blah".

I think we all understand that. That is why I stress it is a good launch point. It also doesn't mean the above is going to happen. My account has been live for over 6 years with no issues. If my account were to go down tomorrow for some unknow reason, guess what? I still have income streams that are not affected by that.

In addition, Amazon doesn't just shut off accounts for no good reason – so unless you are doing something sinister, why worry?

You need to start here on Amazon to dip your toes in the water. It's an amazing place to begin. It's where the customers are, it's where the opportunity is, it's where you can be your own boss and it's where you can work from anywhere. It allows you to scale infinitely. IT'S ALL HERE. Got it?

Now let's dive into the avenue that I personally have the most experience in.

Retail Arbitrage

For the sake of simplicity, I'm just going to assume that the majority of you are newer to being a seller on Amazon. I am also going to assume that many of you are logical and want to try and start something on Amazon with as little risk and money upfront. Does that sound good to you?

Good. Now let's get started!

With my previous assumptions in mind, let me introduce you all to your new friend named Retail Arbitrage.

What is retail arbitrage anyway? The name sounds kind of daunting doesn't it? But in reality, all retail arbitrage is simply buying something for cheap and reselling it for more.

Retail arbitrage (RA) has been around forever and it continues to grow in volume of dollars. There is a huge surge due to platforms like Amazon and eBay.

With RA, you don't have to go through the hassle of finding your own product. You don't need to stay up late nights speaking with suppliers in China that have fake American names like Sally, Eric, and John (I won't get into why).

You don't have to deal with customs. You don't have to lay awake at night hoping your product makes it to the shore and your money is safe in some stranger's hands you've never met.

Oh, and best of all – you do not need to spend a PENNY on advertising, which is huge.

When I was first starting out, I went straight to private label thinking that retail arbitrage had a negative connotation to it.

I didn't want to be the guy who was out digging through bins at a Goodwill, or raiding a thrift store or a garage sale on the weekends. In addition, I valued my time off from corporate too much.

It wasn't that I was scared of being judged per se, it was that I didn't see how I could easily scale that business model at the time.

I was also leaving my house at 6:00am every morning to commute into the city and was not home until 7pm most nights.

I literally did not have the actual free time to invest during the weekdays and if I had tried to go out all weekend and search for product, my wife would have probably killed me or left me.

Luckily for me, what I did have going for me at the time was money in the bank.

Private label at the time just made sense for me, and I fit that individual who is ideal to start a private label business.

You all need to be honest with yourself, if you are someone who has a big ego or cares about what other people think of them, retail arbitrage may be a hard pill for you to swallow. Personally, I don't think anyone is too good to do any type of job. I have been a busboy, I have been a bartender, I have done catering, I have scooped ice cream, heck I have done it all.

If anything, it has given me a better perspective on life and has helped me strive for better. It has also given me a higher appreciation for people that work in the service industry and other related industries where you get little pay and do lots of physical labor.

Retail arbitrage is such a broad category with so many different opportunities within it. You can buy and sell antiques, you can sell clothing, you can sell books, DVDs, CDs, video game systems, videos, etc.

There are so many cool new pieces of software out there that make the process of retail arbitrage very efficient. There is a suite of mobile apps that will instantly tell you the value of an item when you scan the barcode on the box.

Who would've thought that in seconds you can know how much profit down to the penny you will make selling something after your fulfillment costs, shipping, and purchase price? What an amazing world we live in today.

Currently, I sell physical books, DVDs, CDs, and video games as my main source of retail arbitrage. I also sell a couple of board games and audio books. I'll never forget when I scanned my first book and it turned green (green means a profitable book).

I was instantly hooked. There are so many days when I am out scanning books where I purely enjoy what I do, so much so, that I forget to eat all day.

To this day, I still get completely fired up when I see books everywhere I go.

During our last vacation we were back in my hometown of Santa Barbara, CA and we stopped at a local farmer's market down the street from our Airbnb.

As we were exiting my wife noticed a sign that said "free books" from afar. When we turned the corner there were seven full boxes of newer looking books just sitting there for free!

We pulled $75 in profit out of it immediately and kept going on about our day. As we were walking away, I looked over at my father-in-law and said "This is no different than people throwing cash into boxes for me to bring home!" We both laughed – pretty amazing isn't it?

I strongly recommend that if you are going to get into retail arbitrage, you start with something like books. Let me spend a minute explaining something very interesting I have come to find about selling books.

People treat books like they are literally trash. In other words, they don't value them very highly. You would be amazed how many people give books away. That is why Goodwill and Salvation Army have so many books!

That is how the title of my book came to be. I'm sure you've heard the old saying - "One man's trash is another man's treasure."

There are millions of people like me that value books very highly and will pay to get a good price on a used book. Make no mistake, physical books are not going ANYWHERE soon. They are in very high demand and are here to stay.

Do any of you remember when Amazon first got started over two decades ago? Do you remember what they were in the beginning? An online bookstore!!! People forget that.

Jeff Bezos said in an interview that the best product in the world to sell are books. That is due to each book being its own product or SKU, and there are millions of different books out there in the world. So, in this category alone, you have millions of options to sell.

Just think of the availability that provides you for not only scale, but repeat buyers and vertical integration. If you have the software and processes down for one type of book, you have it for them all!

The listing, the prepping, and the packaging is all going to be stream-lined.

Initially, I thought long and hard about sharing information on sourcing books with other people as it would saturate the market, but the sad reality is that most people who are reading this book will not take action on what I am sharing, which is unfortunate for them.

On top of all that, most people that get into books move onto other shiny objects once they get bored. Sound familiar?

In fact, I believe for most of you, you WILL move on for any number of reasons, but books will be your launch pad for success. That is totally fine!

What recently hit me was that if it weren't for someone else like me, I never would've found out about this in the first place. I owe it to others to tell them my experience.

It has had such a positive impact in my life that it would be a shame for me not to share it with a couple more people where it can do the same for them.

It really is true when people say that only about 1% of the people who learn about a new opportunity actually take advantage of it. That obviously goes back to people that chase ideas/fads and hop from one thing to the next.

Everyone wants to make the quick buck. It's not enough to just read something and daydream about it all day, never taking action to make it a reality.

Those same people will go through life working a job they hate, and constantly live for the weekend. It's not a life worth living. It's no surprise why so many people like this live through celebrities and sports superstars.

It's so funny how they know all the latest gossip and all their game highlights and stats. They think that person's life is way more exciting!! Why not live your own best life instead?

I don't watch sports at all. I simply don't have the time. I'm out there trying to improve myself and grow my business any chance I get. There are only so many hours in the day.

Here is my underlying theory on building up income streams on Amazon. Think of retail arbitrage as your income foundation. You have to work hard at it to build it up, but once you get it rolling it can fund and open the door to other opportunities such as private label.

Since private label can be capital intensive, your retail arbitrage efforts/profits can go towards building your own private label brand over time. The risk and level of capital investment that goes into retail arbitrage is nowhere near that of private label.

You see, if you're spending a ton doing retail arbitrage, you're simply doing it wrong. You are finding items at places where you should not be paying any more than pennies on the dollar. For example, I typically get all my books for less than $0.50. If I'm paying $1.00 or more, that's pretty high for me since I buy mostly in bulk now.

Based on my personal numbers I'm getting anywhere from a 1,000%-1,200% return per book. Buying and selling like that will be common for you on your retail arbitrage journey IF YOU BUY RIGHT, THAT is the key.

You can quickly build up capital like that, and you will have minimal investment up front.

My Route/The Ideal Route

It turns out that the path I ended up taking turned out to be a pretty good one. The growth was steady, I didn't have many setbacks, and the risk was minimal. I suggest you try going a similar route that I did.

Below I noted for each of you where I was in my journey, as well as the associated sales numbers to give you the clearest picture of each transition.

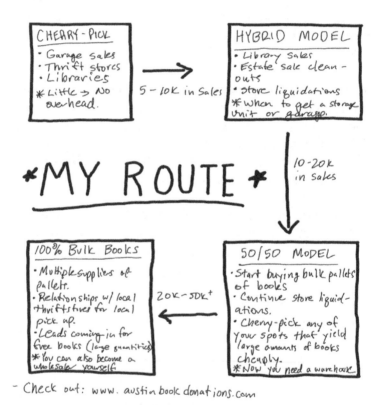

CHERRY - PICK
- Garage sales
- Thrift stores
- Libraries
* Little → No overhead.

5 - 10k in Sales →

HYBRID MODEL
- Library Sales
- Estate sale clean-outs
- Store liquidations
* When to get a storage unit or a garage.

10-20k in sales

MY ROUTE

50/50 MODEL
- Start buying bulk pallets of books
- Continue store liquidations.
- Cherry-pick any of your spots that yield large amounts of books cheaply.
* Now you need a warehouse.

20k - 50k+ ←

100% Bulk Books
- Multiple suppliers of pallets.
- Relationships w/ local thrift stores for local pick up.
- Leads coming in for free books (large quantities)
* You can also become a wholesaler yourself.

- Check out: www. austin book donations.com

This next segment is only meant to be a quick birds-eye view. We will get deeper into each of these in later chapters.

Cherry-Picking Books

"Cherry-Picking" books is simply going out and buying books individually, at various locations where you can actually see the value of the books before you buy them.
In the beginning, all you need to focus on is cherry-picking books at places like garage sales, thrift stores, libraries, etc.

The best way to do this is always by getting on google maps and searching up something like "thrift stores near me".

While you are doing this, you are going to want to start making contacts with managers of these stores. Over time, you will most likely be able to cultivate these relationships into larger lead sources when you have space to take on more inventory.

It's not uncommon to find a local thrift store that can start giving you a pallet or two a week of their overflow product.

At this stage, your overhead is going to be extremely low.

You will be doing everything out of your garage or office, and hopefully be keeping a clean working space.

I recommend buying shelving or a rack like this one to the right at Home Depot. It is super durable and can hold over 1,000 lbs.

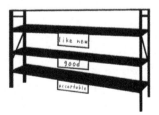

Throw some cardboard on the top of each rack so it does not indent your books.

Each rack will hold different types of book conditions. Lowest quality will be labeled "acceptable," middle quality is "good," and top quality is "like new."

You will be sending all your books to be fulfilled by Amazon. This is also known as FBA. That means that the minute you can ship out a box of books, you want to get it shipped and out of the way.

Don't let books pile up. Remember, when inventory is sitting unprocessed it's costing you money.

Keep at this until your sales get to $5,000-$10,000 a month. I would recommend getting closer to $10,000.

From here you will start to get some traction and want to start looking into more of a hybrid model.

Hybrid Model

At the $10,000 mark you will most likely start to see some sort or resistance or flattening of your sales if you stay with the current model of cherry-picking. Most of this is due to the maximum leverage of your time. You only have so many hours in the day. In addition, your local sources may start to get exhausted.

This is when you need to start thinking about how to maximize your time. This is when you need to use leverage to get your hands on a lot of product.

At this point, you are going to want to incorporate library sales, estate sales, and lead generation for larger book removals on places like Craigslist and Facebook marketplace.

Some of you may be wondering why you wouldn't just start out by doing this in the first place and skipping cherry-picking all together.

I believe it is of absolute importance to get your "reps in". You need to understand the software over time.

You need to get a feel for what sells well and what doesn't. You need to get your scanning and listing methods down.

There is no reason to rush through all this - it's a short amount of time and the learning curve isn't steep. Don't worry, you'll get there.

Before jumping from your garage or storage unit into a warehouse, I recommend that you are doing at least $20,000 a month in sales using this model.

The 50/50 Model

You want to be able to use your existing cash-flow to fund as much of the operations in your new warehouse as possible. Do not keep piling unnecessary overhead onto your business.

This is when you are going to start using some of the contacts of the managers you have gathered from some of your thrifting/library locations.

Do they have location distribution centers where they store excess inventory to sell by the pound? What do the libraries do with all their excess materials? Who is the best person for me to call to set something up?

You will be buying larger volumes of books, sight unseen for the most part since you are buying them by the pound. You will be buying off liquidation sites, government education sites, etc. These will be named for you later.

Hopefully you own a larger SUV, since this will really come in handy at this point. For others, you will be renting a 16-foot box truck for most of your pick-ups.

When you get to the $20,000+ mark, you are again going to realize that scaling to the next level is going to be hard unless you make another transition in your business model.

The way I like to think of the shift is like this – Up until this point, you have gone to get all the books yourself.

You drove all of over town to all the thrift stores.

You traveled far to library sales and maybe estate sales. You went and picked up larger book lots from your leads off of several marketplaces.

You made trips to liquidation centers and school district overflow distribution centers. Boy, it gets exhausting.

However, it's time to get all the books to come to YOU. This is the major shift. This is when you start buying bulk books by the pallet. Although this initially feels great and you get to drive less, your overhead will start to creep up on you.

Bulk Books

This is when your warehouse costs start and your constant purchase of large amounts of books (book burn) kicks in.

At this point, I easily spend up to $5,400 a week on books. For many of you that may be your cost for books for the first four months or more in the beginning.

What you are going to quickly realize is that you are going to immediately take home less profit the minute you transition into a warehouse. That is because initially your top line (sales) will stay the same, and your bottom line (profits), will take a nose dive.

Do not freak out when this happens as it is natural with any business as you scale up. Soon after you make the transition, you will start to see the fruits of your labor, as long as you are consistent. There is always a lag time to see the benefits of the effort you are putting in today.

I always say that the work you put in today, you won't see reflecting in your sales at least 30 days from now.

Conversely, the sales you are seeing today, are a result of what you did 30 days ago.

I recently got off a phone call with a gentleman that I mentor that was frustrated by what little progress he was seeing for that day in his seller app.

He told me how hard he had been working all week and how many books he was able to source and list. I already knew what the problem was right from the get-go.

"Didn't you have 0 employees a month ago? Wasn't this around the time you were hardly working? Remember that trip you went on?"

He had not been consistent what-so-ever in the past 30 days and it was showing. Even though he was working hard the last couple days, how could that effort be evident yet in his numbers?

The work he is doing now, pays off later. Point being, you must always be **consistent** with sending in product. It's a numbers game.

Once you have a warehouse you should have at least three types of book source funnels.

1. Bulk books by the pound from large vendors.
2. Inbound lead generation from your own website.
3. Local pick-ups or drop offs from mom-and-pop stores.

Now that you have a snap shot of what my path looked like, lets jump into other important factors you'd better think about before pulling the trigger on anything.

PART THREE: RESEARCH

Remember this word carefully – due diligence. You need to do your due diligence and research before you do anything worthwhile in your life.

There are a few important topics that we must cover relating to doing your due diligence that are absolutely essential to starting your business.

Proximity

I can't express the importance of proximity when it comes to selecting a warehouse or storage unit. When talking about proximity, there are several different aspects to it.

It turns out that some people will have a geographic advantage over others when it comes to this type of business.

Let's talk about some different types of proximity factors that you'll want to look into before choosing a warehouse/storage unit.

Here are the types of questions you'll want to start asking yourself as you start to think about proximity.

Are there any book donations suppliers near me?
How about major thrift store chains?
Do you live near any major "shipping lanes"?
Am I located near any landfills?
Are any major truck rental companies nearby?

If you can't find any suppliers on Google Maps in your area, it's going to make things a bit tough.

You're going to be doing a lot more driving to not only acquire sources in the beginning, but have to drive further each time you are ready to pick up more supply.

That means more time, more gas, and more money. There is a definite opportunity cost that you have to weigh when looking for a place to operate.

Also, if you are going to hire/schedule freight to pick up your books for you, you're going to be paying much more if they have to go hours further (especially if they cross state lines).

The cheaper, rundown warehouse outside of the city limits may not be your best option even if it's going to save you a couple bucks. You need to run the numbers!

If you live in a large city like I do, if you hit traffic going to and from work, that could easily cost you 2 hours a day of your time and productivity. It can also start to drain on you mentally and physically. Think opportunity cost again.

Other things you need to consider are how close rental truck companies are located to your spot. You will undoubtedly have to rent trucks over and over again for various reasons. We typically rented once per week for the longest time.

Look for either Penske, Enterprise, or Ryder. My favorite of the three is Penske. They have provided me the best rates over time and are almost always able to provide me with a good working truck.

When I got into my first warehouse, I looked at all these factors. I was literally MINUTES from two different sources. I was also located right on the main highway so that I could easily get in and out of town.

On top of that, I was located right on one of the major shipping lanes, so my inbound shipments to Amazon were dirt cheap. For everyday supplies, Home Depot was located right down the street, and I had a recycling center close by.

This was an ideal spot, but we eventually outgrew that location.

What is important to note is that we absolutely maximized that space to the point where it <u>almost</u> started to hurt us. That's when we knew it was time to leave. Staying there would have cost us money in the form of lost opportunities.

If you end up starting out in a warehouse (which I don't recommend), or upgrading into one later, there are going to be key vendors you will need to provide you with constant, uninterrupted service or else it will cripple your business.

Selecting Vendors

Internet

Do yourself a favor and do NOT bypass doing your research when it comes to looking into vendor services for your business.

When we had selected a certain internet provider in the past, it turned to be a nightmare. It wasn't until after the service provider had already installed their service and had been paid, that we realized the mistake we had made.

To make matters worse, that same internet company actually didn't have service there at all, they outsourced the service to some small internet company in town which basically provided us with dial-up!

Needless to say, I wasted several days of production and had a nice splitting headache from several long phone calls. Of course, there were the unnecessary expenses as well.

In the end, we were able to switch to a larger provider that had great internet speed for our scanning and listing activities.

For reference, the internet we have now is 600 mbps. Prior, it was 8-16 mbps…LOL. Oh, and it costs us the same price.

We currently have business internet and phone for $115/month through Spectrum. If you feel you don't need a business line it's going to be a tad cheaper.

By the way, if you are deciding to use your same service provider that you have at your home, you can expect them to double your service cost for the same internet just because its commercial.

For our situation this ended up being the case, although I was able to negotiate a small price decrease because we were already residential customers of theirs.

Waste Management

Trash is something you can't escape when you are sorting through pallets of books. Sometimes when you buy raw pallets, almost half of a pallet can be trash in some form or another.

Random items such as shoes, VHS, and golf clubs can be found inside these pallets. Trash adds up FAST.

One of the most important things to look for in a warehouse spot is if they have pre-existing trash service.

Make sure it's a large dumpster and find out how often it is hauled away. Once a week will not be enough for most of you. You will want it hauled off 2-3 times a week at least.

Currently we are scheduled for twice a week. Added visits are not much more if you ever need to increase your pick-up frequency.

At the time of this writing, we are paying right around $190/month. Let me contrast this by telling you how much it costs if we were to take this to the dump ourselves.

First, you would have to rent a box truck. Then the fee per ton at the local dump is $55/ton. If you have 12 pallets of trash, that is roughly 6 tons of trash. Approximately $330.

On top of that, if you want to save your pallet and gaylord (which is about an $18 credit back to your supplier), you would have to spent at least an hour or more to pull the trash out and try and salvage the box and pallets.

Otherwise, they will just push the whole pallet over the edge into the dump and you will be unable to get your supplies back. That's another $216 dollars of lost money in your pocket ($18 per pallet/gaylord x 12).

So, all in you're looking at $546 dollars just for one trip to the dump in expenses and lost savings. This is how much trash we usually have in just one week.

So now multiple that times 4. Now you're really starting to add up expenses. We haven't even factored in the truck rental price yet for all this.

Get my point? Find a good, affordable trash service. It may sting a little to pay for waste pick up, but it is certainly a lesser evil of the two options.

My last point to add is simply this – our first warehouse had free waste services. We had access to two large dumpsters and they were picked up three times a week!

Thinking back on the volume we were doing then, that was at least saving us $400 a week in waste costs, or $1,600 a month. You need to factor this type of savings in when you're looking for your first warehouse spot.

If you are looking at storage units or working out of your garage, it's going to be tough to deal with that kind of trash. You won't have as much, but you certainly will have a decent amount.

Some storage unit facilities will have access to a dumpster and some won't. Please do your homework first. You need to be researching everything.

Payments and Setting Up Vendor Accounts

You must always provide your media vendors with a Sales Tax ID and some additional paperwork beforehand. With that being said, you'd better already have a Sales Tax ID with your business name or sole proprietor info on it.

Without that, they won't accept you as a vendor and you will look like a real noob when they ask you what is taking so long to return the paperwork.

Be prepared to also wire money for transactions with larger reputable companies.

On test runs you can usually get away with using your credit card for the small one-time purchase, but for full semi-truck loads a wire is usually favored (that way they don't pay processing fees on those high amounts).

Personally, I love to try and see if I can pay by credit card with these vendors as much as possible. It allows me to float payment longer, and I get 1.5% cash back on all my purchases. That really adds up.

It's not uncommon for me to get about $250 a month in cash back rewards. That's $3,000 a year in cash back. That's a lot of golf.

Trucking Services

Trucking is one of the costs that can really sneak up on you at the end of any month.

Back in the day, I would sit there analyzing our P & L statements and be blown away with how much we had to pay towards trucking.

However, as time went on, we were able to finally get some leverage with our current trucking rental company (Penske), in order to continue to bring down our rental rates.

At the time of this writing, we are paying the following for the two types of trucks we rent:

26-footer /w liftgate - $90/day + .12 a mile
16-footer /w liftgate - $60/day + .12 a mile

Looking back, I should have demanded these rates earlier on due to the frequency that we were going to be using their vehicles, but I felt like we were too small to have any negotiation power. It turns out I was wrong.

I remember the conversation pretty clearly the day that negotiation on our rates took effect. I wish I could say I did it strategically, but it was pure happenstance.

I was using Enterprise Truck Rental from day one. I quickly realized that they never seemed to have the truck I needed due to low inventory.

On top of that, when I upgraded to 26-footers they didn't have one available, so I was forced to go grab one from Penske.

On the day the negotiation took place, I had called Enterprise to find out if they had a 16-footer for this particular pick up, as they were located closer to our warehouse.

They happened to have one on hand. I told Penske to cancel my rental that I had made a reservation for and when they asked me why, I told them I was getting one from Enterprise.

Boy, did they not want that to happen! They dropped the rental from $115/day to $90/day and lowered the mileage on the spot just to get one from them immediately.

They then said they were going to have their rep reach out to me since they noticed my volume of rentals was quite frequent.

Needless to say, I rented from them that day and have used them ever since.

Last note on trucking (which is an important one). Every time you rent a truck from a place like Penske you are required to be insured.

By having business insurance, you can save yourself up to $60 per rental by providing your own insurance on file with them. That was something else I wish I had known sooner. I estimate I could have saved at least $1,000 from that little piece of info.

The way I ultimately found this out was by simply asking questions regarding all the line items on the statements.

If you haven't already done this, or you are going to start renting trucks soon, this little piece of info just gave you a 100x return on your investment in this book ☺.

When you move into bulk and you are getting semi deliveries ranging from 40-48 pallets at a time, you should be doing a lot less driving.

Remember, the books are going to be coming to you for the most part! For semi loads, I was lucky enough to find a reliable owner/operator truck driver who owns his own rig.

Because of him, I get reliable/cheap service around the clock, and he gets continuous shipments from me.

If I am buying out of state, I utilize Uber trucking (which has been a great experience).

You typically get the lowest rate and the drivers are vetted and have scores attached to their name or company.

Now that you have an understanding as to what vendors you will need to get set up with, lets dive into getting prepared for this business from a mental standpoint.

Keep Your Head in The Game.

I don't know what people expect when they are looking to start a new endeavor. It's quite absurd, really. It's like they think they can just think happy, positive thoughts and make all their dreams come true while lying on the couch with a bag of Doritos on their stomach.

Starting your own Amazon business, or any kind of business for that matter, is like moving a mountain. It's so incredibly tough to start and grow a successful one.

There are several books on the subject - none that are worth mentioning, because so much of it is simply not helpful. You can read all you want, but unless you take action and learn as you are DOING it, you're not going to make it.

Remember it's all up to YOU. No one is going to carry you across the finish line.

Everyone seems to mention books such as ***think and grow rich*** by Napolean Hill. While this is certainly a good book, its worthless if you just read it over and over and don't implement it. It's also purely a mindset book. It's meant to help you train yourself to think a certain way. This never happens overnight, it's a lifelong endeavor.

You may think that's an obvious observation, but if it was actually being implemented wouldn't there be tens of millions more successful people on the planet?

You want to know what's funny? The same people that read all those books day in and day out are why I'm in business.

Those entrepreneurial/self-help genres sell great and are always found soon after at garage sales and Goodwill's for me to pick up and profit from.

Many of them are selling pipe dreams.

Don't misunderstand me - reading is great, but reading only gets you so far. Especially if you read complete nonsense.

Make no mistake, when you start your book journey it's going to be tough.

With that being said, if you take the information I give you and run with it, full speed ahead – after two years, you should be running a nice, profitable business that you own and no one to answer to but yourself.

You heard me right. And guess what? There is a catch. At times your knees and back are going to ache, and your vehicle may look like a homeless person's car on any given day of the week.

But don't worry – once you start working smart, using machinery, and hiring, you can start to give your body and your car a rest.

Let me ask you this, would you rather keep doing the same old 9-5 every day that you hate, or give something new a try that brings on new and exciting adventures every day? It really is like searching for treasure all day - I love the thrill of the hunt!

To some people two years seems like a very long time. In the scheme of things, it's really nothing. If you knew you could live off this income stream full time in that short time frame, wouldn't you do everything you could to make it happen?

For those of you that aren't scared, read on because this is where I give you all the additional information you need. We're going to talk strategy for sourcing, software, hardware, you name it.

This book isn't based on theory. This is a book is based on tried-and-true experience. I provide you with everything you need to get going. I am literally telling you what to do. Get out there and get those books!

Before we start – I highly recommend that you take this same route.

If you go the route I did. You will ensure a number of things. First you will know for certain if you enjoy this type of business and all it entails.

Second, the financial risk is so minimal to get started. You should be able to use your cash flow to help take things to the next level if you so choose (going bulk).

Now, let's talk about why I love books. Books are everywhere. There are billions of physical books out there in the world. There are so many ways to come by books, it's hard not to run into them. It's such a plentiful source, yet they are still in such high demand.

Whoever said print books are dead was so wrong. Tell that to all the book resellers making a full time living off books alone.

So, where are the best sources? The obvious answer is commonly wherever you can get your books the cheapest. But that's only half the battle, because you need volume as well.

What you need are dozens of sources at your fingertips that you can constantly cycle through without running out.

Let me start by saying that if you live in a larger city and are close to colleges, you are going to have a much easier time finding books by default, thus you have a huge advantage.

Mapping Out Where to Source

A great place to start is to get on Google Maps and search up the following stores: Savers, Goodwill, any thrift store chains, libraries, etc. Take inventory of what is closest to you and get a good schedule down of when you are going to be hitting these locations.

You should always take a quick note of the date you visited a certain location, the current color of the sticker on the book (usually a date), and time of day.

If you're lucky, you have a car that is good on gas. Make no mistake, you will put mileage on that vehicle and spend plenty of money on gas.

By the way, gas is something you can't ignore when factoring your expenses. If you aren't calculating that, you are leaving out key expenses and conducting bad business.

Take the time to strategically plot out your sourcing time so that it is efficient from a gas AND time perspective.
Also, worth mentioning – You need to keep a tab on how many miles you are driving a day so you can write it off!

Simply start an excel spreadsheet so that you can update it daily. If you get the app on your phone you can easily access this and put in that data. Currently, the write off amount is .58/mile as of 2019.

Talk to the staff

When you frequent these places, you need to start talking. What I mean is that you need to be friendly right off the bat. Get to know these people at these different stores.

Remember what days they work. Find out a few things about them. These are the people that are going to give you a heads up on when books are put out. They may even give you "backroom access," meaning you can go into the back and scan the books before they are put onto the floor.

Pro Tip: Don't go up to staff on day one like you own the place asking for when they put out books, etc. Put in some time along the way and build those relationships. You don't want to ruin any good sources that are close by you because you're acting like a turd.

Remember, first impressions are everything. They are going to remember you if you sounded like you had no idea what you were talking about, or started making ridiculous requests right up front.

In my experience, the majority of people working at these places who see you consistently buying lots of books get naturally curious about what you are doing. They will eventually approach you asking what it is that you do with all the books.

In fact, one of the last times I was in a Goodwill I was asked by the cashier if I owned a bookstore since I always bought so many books.

That is one of the best things anyone could ask you. It opens up the flood gates of beneficial conversation & an open line of communication that could greatly benefit you.

One last thing on this. Don't just "talk business" to these people all the time. You should care about these people that you are interacting with that you get to know over time. You should want to know how their weekend was or how their kids are doing. It will not serve you to put all that past you and just focus on making money.

Most people can hone in on that very easily and it won't be a good look for you. People want to do business with people that they like and get along with.

Most times, they will even take less money from someone that they like instead of more money from someone they don't like or mistrust. Remember that!

Ask for A Deal.

Recently I went on a trip back to Santa Barbara, CA to visit family and my wife had an affiliate conference she was attending at a local hotel on the beach.

Since my brother is now selling books part-time, I figured he and I should go out for a day and go on a little sourcing road trip.

One of the first Goodwill locations we stopped at was a goldmine. We got over 50 books within 30-45 mins. Knowing full well from past experience from trial and error, I was fully prepared to do whatever I could to get a discount on the books we had picked up.

Approaching the register to pay, I identified the manager who turned out to be a nice guy and introduced myself and my brother, letting him know I was a larger bulk book buyer out in Austin, TX.

He warmed up to us quick and let us know when this location typically put out the books (obviously a valuable tip), he even invited us to come back later that day to look over the new books he was going to put out (unfortunately we couldn't make it back that day).

On top of it all, I asked him for a discount since we were buying so many right then, and that my brother would be a regular customer. Without hesitation he exclaimed, "I don't normally do this, but let me see what I can do for you." And just like that, he offered us 50% off of every single paper back we bought.

Make it a regular habit to ask for a discount every time. Get creative. Think outside the box. Let me give you another example that would be geared towards buying a private seller's books (aka a neighborhood pickup).

Let's assume you went to a potential customer's home that had 500 books that they wanted to get rid of.

After quickly going through their collection, you determine (through your scanning software) that you can take 125 of them since they are green/accepts.

After negotiating the price on the 125 books, you simply ask what they will be doing with the remainder of the other books. They tell you that if they don't sell, they will be taking them down to the local Goodwill for a donation.

Right then and there you could offer to take them all off their hands so that they wouldn't have to make that trip themselves and pack up several heavy boxes to lug away.

They most certainly will take you up on this offer, knowing full well that they don't want to do that themselves. Now that's VALUE.

That is what I mean about thinking outside of the box. 99% of the time that person will take you up on that offer and be happy to get those books out of their hair. By the way, those 375 books you could take to somewhere like half-priced books and make another $100 right off the bat. Food for thought.

You may not have a half-priced books near you, but look for a similar outfit that will pay you for your duds (AKA the books you can't sell). If you can't find brick and mortar stores to take them, you can go to online and find buyback companies websites such as sellbackyourbook.com.

Get There First

I can't stress enough how important being punctual is in this book game. Often times if you are even 5 minutes late to an event, store, or garage sale you could be missing hundreds of dollars just like that.

If anything, you'll want to be early. Do whatever you have to. Set your clock forward, get in the habit of being there early, and get good with alerts to give you ample time to get to your destination.

Personally, I set my watch forward 10 minutes, which seems to work well for me. If there is anything that comes up that I was not anticipating, I have a nice buffer.

 Remember, you wouldn't be late to something as important as your own wedding, so don't be late when it is time to provide for yourself or your family!

Oh, and something else regarding getting there first...

Don't ever assume that because someone got to a location or opportunity before you that they know what they are doing. That goes for so many different situations.

A few times throughout my journey I came across other people scanning books at locations prior to me arriving there.

Much to my surprise, 9 times out of 10, I noticed they did not do that good of a job.

PART FOUR: EXECUTION

Building on A Solid Foundation

No matter where you are at this point in your journey, you need to start by building a foundational supply as fast as you can.

A foundational supply simply means an acceptable amount of supply that will provide you with the cash flow you need to continue to purchase books using the cash flow from your business.

For me, I hit my "foundational supply" around 5 months of sourcing (I had an inventory of about 3,500-4,000 books in Amazon FBA at that time).

By the way, this inventory level should be easily attainable while working out of your garage or storage unit (think cherry-picking/hybrid models).

This can even be done in your living room, office, or bedroom. Since you will be sending in your product via Amazon FBA, you won't be storing a ton of books at your house.

Once they are processed and listed, they will get sent out to Amazon's warehouse for storage until they sell.

Worth noting: I was also working full-time at our coffee shop throughout the whole process, so I was able to build that supply up part-time, from about 2pm-5pm during my time off.

If you are able to put more time than I did at that part in your journey, you can get to a foundational supply much sooner.

What you need to do is start by looking at larger chain stores, as they are going to be the most prominent and will also be low hanging fruit. Goodwill, Savers, Thrift Land, and libraries will act as a good base for you to get a consistent number of books at a medium ranged price.

You will be paying more than I pay (since I am a bulk buyer), but it's worth doing to make contacts, get the hang of things, and get your inventory levels up. It's all about making tweaks along the way and adjusting your methods as you go.

Upon your first visit to these places you need to document everything. I kept an excel spreadsheet app on my phone, which was very easy to access.

I typically kept four pieces of information on my excel sheet: source name, managers name, when they put out books, and my last visit to them.

Source	Manager's Name	Day/time they typically put out books	Last Visit on:
Goodwill -Ben White	Sherry	Saturday morning	12-Apr
Goodwill - Manchaca	Bob	Tuesdays	12-Apr
Savers - Downtown	Jim	Wednesday	13-Apr
Thriftland - Stassney	Dale	Wednesday	13-Apr
Goodwill - Beecave	Monica	Friday afternoon	13-Apr

If it's your first time at a new location, you need to scan every book that could be a potential profit.

That means that every single book in the non-fiction section. Stay away from fiction to start. Self-help, cooking, how-to, history, art, textbooks, and many other categories should be getting scanned.

In places such as Goodwill, they put dated stickers on all their books. That means that once you have scanned them initially (on your first visit), you can be very efficient when you go back in and only have to scan the newly dated books.

All these stickers are color coded as well, so it makes things incredibly easy! This will save you a ton of time and headache.

If you live in, or near and larger city, make sure and Google a "Goodwill outlet" and make a stop there.

That was one of my best sources in the beginning. I was able to get 5 books for $1.

That place allowed me to buy thousands of books at rock bottom prices and provided me with a nice margin. When you buy books for $0.20 and can resell them for up to $200, there is a lot of meat on the bone.

Garage sales and estate sales can also be as cheap if you buy right.

PRO-TIP: Don't be afraid to ask employee's and even the manager what day + time they typically put out the books! Find out the manager's names and let them know what you do! Always ask if they know who the manager is of their location distribution center for a possible bulk contact.

Inexpensive Supply Sources

This can be a much faster route to building up a foundational supply, since you can essentially find larger quantities of books at a faster rate.

Personally, I love garage sales and estate sales. There is nothing like a good old-fashioned garage sale to go to on Saturday and Sunday.

You can always get the best prices during a garage sale if you play your cards right. You always want to go in and ask for the prices per book upfront before you do any looking around.

You want to do that for two reasons. The first reason is that they might be selling their books for cheaper than you will offer.

Second, is that if you find multiple books that you want to buy, you can offer a lump sum and get a cheaper price per book for the entire lot that you purchase.

Let me give you an example: Let's say I walk into a sale and immediately spot a decent number of books in a back corner. I then go and find the owner and ask her how much per book, she responds by saying they are $1/book.

I say thank you and go over to scan them. Let's say I grab 25 books that are green and go to pay. 9 times out of 10, she would say $25, for which I would immediately say back, "would you do $10 for all of them?". Their response, "Ya sure, why not." It works like a charm. It is also not uncomfortable at all.

You need to realize that for these people, most of the stuff they have for sale is junk to them. Hence the name of my book. Remember, one man's trash is another man's treasure.

They WANT their books sold. If they don't sell, they have to put it right back into their garage. If it's an estate sale, you have even more leverage because then they won't be putting it back at all! They will need to pay for a company to pick up the goods, or haul all that over to the nearest Goodwill.

No matter where you are going to find sources for books, the more leads the better. You need to have as many lead generating sources as possible. You never know when one source is going to go down or dry up.

If your best source dries up and you don't have others to replace it, you're going to be in serious trouble. This has happened to me with my bulk business before, which sent me scrambling for another source!

Currently I do continuous posts on the following apps: Craigslist, Letgo, Nextdoor, Facebook marketplace, and Offer

Up. Between all five of these lead generation platforms I have dings constantly on my phone of someone messaging me. I post weekly and keep everything fresh so that my leads are fresh!

In order to do this seamlessly, you need to create simple and clear templates that you can repeatedly copy and paste into these various apps.

I have a few different templates that I cycle through just to switch things up every now and then.

Below is an example of a template that we use. Keep it short and sweet. Feel free to copy it all you want. Above the bullet point section, I would add a short description above.

Offer things that will entice them to use your service. Free pick up is a great one. Also, due to the current situation we are in, I would add additional safety precautions to the mix.

Make sure you mention that you and your staff will be all showing up with safety gear on, such as a mask and gloves. You need to make your customers feel safe and willing to do business with you.

Another thing we did was have them leave their items either at their door step or in the garage for us so that it was contactless pick-up. Most people appreciate that!

WHAT TYPE OF BOOKS DO WE BUY?

Book Categories that we currently buy:

- Text Books (Academic books)
- Biography / Autobiography / Memoirs
- Self-help
- Entrepreneurial
- Religion
- Travelogues / Travel Literature
- Journalism
- Self-help / Self-improvement
- Guides / Manuals / Handbooks / Technical books

WE BUY BOTH USED AND NEW

SELL MY BOOKS NOW!

By the way, I have tried paid posts on Craigslist and Facebook Marketplace and have NOT found them to be any more effective. Save your money.

When I get messages from sellers coming in from these posts, I have several that I have to vet in order to find a good lead. Many people will only have a handful books to sell or give away, and 99% of the time that is not worth it. You are looking for larger scale book hauls.

It's going to be someone doing spring-cleaning, moving, leftovers from a garage sale, etc.

Do not underestimate how large some of these book hauls can be from homes. One that we did ended up having over 25,000 books in their library. Go figure.

Let's shift gears and talk about where you can find larger lots of books without buying any gaylord pallets.

Quick pause: What, you ask, is a **Gaylord**? A Gaylord box is a large, double-walled cardboard container on a pallet. The name "Gaylord box" has evolved into a generic term for any pallet-sized box for the bulk shipment of books and other types of media. A typical gaylord has anywhere from 800-1200 books in it. They can weigh as much as 1,000-1,200 pounds.

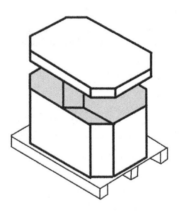

^ **Gaylord box** ^

Larger Supplies of Books

I use the following for bulk deals: booksalefinder.com, Craigslist, and govdeals.com (just to name a few). On these separate platforms you can find a ton of great bulk deals or just loads of books in general at a great price. I can't tell you how many free books I've gotten on Craigslist free section alone.

Booksalefinder.com is mainly where you can go to get the low down on where all the big library sales are in your state.

Library sales can get hairy. Lots of people there don't care about cutting in front of you or straight up grabbing books out of your hand. In these types of events you need to realize they are hectic.

Many of these people go to these sales in order to pay for their next meal, so they tend to not mess around. If you go to one of those you need to bring your A-game.

What does that look like? You need your phone fully charged! Blue tooth scanner at the ready. I would make sure that you also bring a portable charger for your phone or blue tooth scanner, should they get low on battery.

Some blue tooth scanners can go for literally days without a charge, so it is most likely going to be your phone that will need it.

You need something to put books into like a cart or bin as most of these places don't provide this. Make sure that it has wheels.

I recommend bringing a friend or family member along to help you snag books as well. If you get there early enough you may be able to see where the books are placed.

You are also able to join the "friends of the library" group which is very cheap. Usually, that will allow you early access to the books before anyone else.

This is usually a day or two in advance, before anyone else gets to lay eyes on the books.

When the doors do open to a library sale, you shouldn't be running into the fiction section. That is why it is so important to get there early or have early access, so that you can at least map out a game plan.

You're always going to be looking for non-fiction. Art, music, textbooks, business books, entrepreneurship, mental health, motivational, etc.

Those all sell very well, and should be what you are striving to find.

As you get better/more experienced you can even grab books that you believe are good without scanning depending on the situation.

These days I've become so in tune to what sells, that I could do pretty well without any software or scanner. It really all depends how cheap the books are.

At one of my better sources I get them for $.20 a book. At that cost I can afford not to scan the book if I don't want to.

Just for kicks, I've actually tried it before and did very well just picking books up on instinct.

When it comes to govdeals.com, you will most likely need some supplemental equipment to facilitate the transfer of books if you win the bid. It all depends on how many pallets you win and what size car you drive.

For most people you are going to need to rent a truck, even if it's just one larger pallet of books.

Most likely you will need a 16-foot truck with a lift gate. I mainly use a 16-footer (I can fit 6 pallets in there) for smaller pick-ups like this. It really all depends on how large of a lot you win. You will also need a pallet jack if you are dealing with pallets (highly likely). I got mine used for $50 and it works like a champ.

Many times, your car will do just fine if you win one pallet, as long as you have a larger SUV.

Buying Bulk from Larger Vendors.

One small roadblock many sellers can face when trying to go into 100% bulk pallet buying is space constraints and order volume.

Many of these larger vendors typically require a minimum purchase of 40-44 gaylord pallets at a time. That can create a lot of problems for smaller sellers trying to get to the next level.

This is when your garage and storage unit isn't going to cut it anymore. This is why I stress building up your cash flow before you make the jump into a warehouse. With some vendors you may be able to negotiate buying smaller loads for a shorter period of time, with the intention of scaling up with them over time.

There are many vendors that simply won't work with a smaller client due to past experiences. For individuals without supply close by, trucking costs will end up eating up any chance of making a decent margin on product if you try and book smaller loads.

At some point, you WILL have to make the leap over to a warehouse in order to make bulk work.

If you are buying Gaylord's from places like Goodwill at about $40-$60 each for example, it would serve you well to apply for a sales tax exemption.

Sales tax is a very real cost and can pile up fast, raising your cost of goods significantly. If I were to buy a full truck load of gaylords without one, that would be roughly $223 dollars extra in sales tax per load.

If you are buying that many weekly, that is roughly $1,000 per month just in sales tax alone!

All you need for a tax exemption is to bring your sales tax ID number for them. You should already have one of these through the state you operate in since you SHOULD be paying sales tax anyways. Remember, this business is the real deal, so treat it like one.

By the way, Amazon.com collects sales tax for most states on your behalf, so you do not have to deal with that. BUT you still have to claim $0 for your sales tax quarterly. You still have to file even if you owe nothing in sales tax.

PRO-TIP: Call your local state comptroller and have them change your sales tax filing to yearly instead of quarterly as soon as you can.

This will save you lots of time and headache, since the majority of you will only be selling on places like Amazon

---

that collect sales tax. Check your state's status on Amazon to make sure that they do collect.

The Holy Grail

The name of the game at the end of the day is always buy low, sell high. In this business it is easy to get lazy and always go for the low hanging fruit whenever possible, whether it be thrifting or buying bulk gaylords.

Let me tell you, there is a better way. It also happens to be much cheaper.

It takes much more effort and requires time and patience. The million-dollar question you need to ask yourself is this – "How do I become a Goodwill or Salvation Army?"

All these organizations get books for FREE and then they sell them to you. Over the years, all of these organizations have done the ground work of setting up donation infrastructure and logistics in order to make this happen.

You need to stop being the middle man and become first in line to get the product for free.

You can do this several ways.

I recommend creating your own lead-generating website where people can easily visit your site, fill out a form, and then receive an email or call very quickly after submission is done.

I have mine set up on Wix.com. What is great about Wix.com is that they have an app that you can get any communications, such as a lead, straight to your phone instantaneously.

Whenever someone fills out a form, it is sent directly to your app and you can communicate with them directly through that app.

As you can see below, I collect all the relevant information that is needed in order to make contact with them ASAP.

I also have a part where they can tell me what they have for free pick-up. That way I do not waste my time picking up smaller orders. I also do not have to contact them prior to try and find out what they have for pick-up!

^ Website form from my Wix app ^

I love this functionality because it also allows you to store all of your contact forms in one place, so you can easily reply and manage things from that portal.

What is also very handy about wix is how easy their SEO features are (which are also free, by the way). They lead you through making sure your site is optimized for all the keywords you need in order to catch your ideal clients.

By doing this, I have been able to get a ton of leads, all basically for free. I haven't spent a single dollar on ads. I say basically free, because I do have to pay a small monthly fee for the hosting of the site.

If you are interested in creating your own or just curious to check out my site you can visit it at:

http://www.austinbookdonations.com

Another quick and easy way to get free books is by putting up "bandit signs" around town on highly trafficked areas.
A bandit sign is basically a sign you are able to put out for free without paying anyone.

When doing a bandit sign, you want to get your message out as quick and effective as possible. You simply can't put a huge paragraph on a sign and hope it is effective.

You need to be short and to the point. Here are some examples of effective signs:

1. Cash for books (with your phone number underneath)
2. I Buy books (with your phone number underneath)
3. Sell me your books (with your phone number underneath)

Remember – short and sweet. Get the messaging out fast.
These people are zooming by your signs in their cars, you
need to be able to catch their attention quick.

The same thing applies to adding a window decal/sticker to
your car. Using that same messaging on either a window
sticker or a magnetic sign that is placed effectively on your
car. These can be made inexpensively and can make you tons
of money.

In most cases, you will have more calls than you can handle,
so be prepared for a way to organize and execute on all the
leads you are getting.

There is one last creative way that I like which an
acquaintance of mine tried. What he ended up doing was
putting out donation bins around town.

These bins most often are made
out of metal, are bulky, and can
cost a decent amount upfront to
purchase. Of course, once you
do that, they technically last
forever.

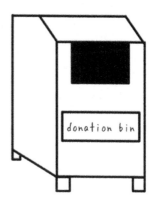

In terms of finding a good spot
for these donation bins, I would
recommend that you drive
around town and see where
other donation companies have
placed their bins.

Are they at gas stations? Churches? Schools? Find out what is
most common, and then use that same methodology to place
yours in other parts of town.

In terms of rent for bins like these, $30-$50/month is a
common amount. Obviously, this will depend where you
have them placed.

Places such as a church may even allow free real estate space
for your donation bin based on the added value it brings its
members and the overall mission of the company that is
placing it there.

Make sure that if you end up building one of these for
yourself you get the dimensions perfect. If you build one
specifically for the size of a Gaylord box that would be ideal.

That way you can simply wheel a pallet and Gaylord box in
and out of the donation bin seamlessly.

> **PRO-TIP:** See if any donation companies have old donation bins they are looking to sell or get rid of. Always make sure they are made of metal or aluminum, never wood-based. You want them to last!

Regardless of how many books you buy, you need to become a great negotiator.

<u>Negotiation</u>

Negotiation is key, no matter what business model you choose.

It is the difference between buying "right" and not being profitable from buying too high.

I will always negotiate whenever I go out to buy books, no matter where it is. That is simply for this ONE reason - it doesn't hurt to take the conversation there for a better price!

Why would you not ask for a better price every time? Don't let your embarrassment, shyness, or lack of preparedness stop you from capitalizing on saving money and building long lasting, profitable relationships.

Before we go on, let's talk about what a real negotiation should look like. It should never be in the form of a WIN-LOSE, unless it is a one-time deal.

What if that person you "took to the cleaners" realized how bad they got cleaned out and decided not to refer you to others or give you repeat business?

Or what if they give you a bad review based on the experience they had from not getting treated fairly.

That could cost you lots of money down the road from people passing your business over for one with better reviews.

My argument here is that your negotiations with larger vendors should always be as close to a WIN-WIN as possible. Let's look at a real-life example I had with one of my bulk contacts.

When I met this gentleman for the first time, I initially sent him over a dozen free, FULL gaylords of duds that I did not have the space for at the time. From these, he was able to make over $1,000 that I provided to him for FREE.

The initial price he offered to me was to sell me gaylords for $0.10/pound. From there I immediately told him what I was accustomed to paying on average, $40 - $75 a gaylord (flat fee).

He immediately said that was too low and if he offered that to me, he would have to offer that to all his other buyers.

That was the point in which I had to quickly think on my feet to help bridge the gap of value for us both.

I identified the fact that although the duds I had brought him before were of no value to me (at the time), he could expect those donations on a regular basis from me. To him, those were worth at least $75 a piece.

Being a reasonable guy, he completely understood that anything I bought from him would be returned right back for him to sell and he would basically be making double his money reselling the gaylords to customers that didn't mind a scanned gaylord.

His new proposal to me was to give me a .03/pound credit for every gaylord I donated to him, to then allow me to buy at .07 a pound.

Now we were getting somewhere. I did add one additional thing on top of that. I asked to have a 1,000 pound "ceiling" to the weight of the gaylord so I could control my costs and cap off at $70 per gaylord. He countered me back saying ok, let's just do $75 flat.

BOOM. Now that's what I call a win-win.

For me, I get to know my exact costs that I will incur on each box, AND I know from several hundred gaylord purchases in the past that even mediocre gaylords still yield me a bunch of profitable books.

Because I watch my numbers like a hawk, I know that on average I net about $6.50 per book. If the average box yields me 60 acceptable books, that is almost $400 in profit. I also monetize many of the additional books by sending them to buyback companies. I knew the risk was low and the reward was high.

On his side, he makes over $1,000 selling back the duds he gets from me (per week) AND gets to make money selling them to me initially as well. Clearly an even bigger win for him in terms of monetary value.

That is what it's all about guys. Clearly, he is benefiting greatly on what I am offering him and because of that, don't you think this relationship will stand the test of time?

Of course, it will! To this day, it is still my most profitable source AND we both bend over backwards for each other whenever one of us gets in a bind.

Do you think that if he has a limited amount of gaylords left, he'll reach out to me before others? Most likely. Why? Because of the tremendous value I have given him and the relationship I will continue to build along the way.

As if that wasn't enough value, I went above and beyond and offered to deliver all the gaylords to him free of cost. That way he would not have to deploy his truck, gas, and two employees to get the job done.

The relationship has continued to evolve overtime benefiting both of us. I now keep all the "duds" and I get to monetize them in several ways on my end! Things couldn't be better. He is also getting more money per pallet from me. Again, a win/win.

This is a perfect Segway into talking about landing your first bulk contacts.

Landing Bulk Clients

When the time is right, I highly recommend that you make a leap to buying in bulk for your book business. In many ways, bulk is superior to going out and sourcing. Even a hybrid model of the two is better.

But, those of you who have no experience sourcing books, I always recommend you start by getting your feet wet with cherry picking.

For anyone who has been in sales during your working career or may have some experience with making calls, you will be at a significant advantage when you initially start on your bulk journey, as "hitting the phones" is going to be your first stop.

The best place to start in landing your first bulk clients is to go on Google Maps on your computer or phone and search in your area for places like the Goodwill outlet, thrift store chains, any mom-and-pop thrift stores, etc.

You are going to be looking anywhere online for places that take some sort of raw donations from people. Raw donations meaning they have constant donations from customers that are not scanned by the company.

PRO-TIP: You want to avoid books that have had the opportunity of being scanned prior to getting into your hands from these sources. If they are not "raw or credential" loads they have been scanned!

FYI – donation places like Goodwill and Salvation Army usually have both scanned and non-scanned resources. Sometimes they are separated and charged accordingly and other times they are lumped in with each other.

As you develop a relationship with these clients you can be more specific with what works best for you and your business.

As long as you are upholding your end of the bargain, they are usually happy to accommodate as long as it's not costing them more in time and labor.

When looking for a source, know that proximity is key. Do not look for places that are hours away from you. This is going to jack up your per box price by adding truck and gas costs.

Another major consideration is your time. Make sure to exhaust/vet every close by resource before you start to go outside your city or state for bulk sources.

For my reader's sake I will tell you that out of every 10 calls that I made, 2-3 would not only have product to sell me, but were interested in working with me.

So, don't think that just because you made three calls and struck out, there is nothing out there. Like anything else worthwhile, you're going to have to put in the time.

You should keep a spreadsheet somewhere safe that has a big contact list of bulk sources that you can pull from when in need. Over time, you will find out which sources seem to have the best ROI. That doesn't mean you should write off the other sources on the list.

Always keep that spreadsheet handy (and growing) just in case you need a new source for a rainy day. You never know when a source will run dry (this has happened to me and I learned from it!).

I'm going to make this as easy as possible for you guys. I will be providing all the ammo you need to go into these calls well equipped with confidence and a clear path to victory.

Let's start with what price you should aim to pay to make your business profitable.

I have purchased thousands of gaylords and I have been religious with keeping the raw data from all of them. What I have determined is that unless you are buying full semi's full of gaylords (about 48 at a time), paying $65-$75/gaylord is a baseline average for you to go off ($40-$60 a gaylord if you are buying 48 at a time/18-wheeler full).

If you are paying $75 or less for your gaylords you are doing great. Plenty of my viewers on my YouTube channel and Instagram often relay to me that they pay up to $200-$250 per pallet.

Even if those gaylords end up being profitable, usually the margins aren't high enough to justify your time invested and ultimately you won't be able to build a profitable book business paying that much for gaylords. You have to buy right – buying right is essential. Like many other businesses in life, you make the money when you buy.

Important note: $75 does not include the costs of a truck built in. After those costs it typically is $80-$85/gaylord depending on how much you pick up at one time.

Most of our shipments these days are semi-truck loads coming in. This will add about $8-$10 on top of pallet price.

However, we do have smaller vendors that provide exceptional quality, so we still like to buy those as well.

When we do this, we will get no less than 12 pallets from these guys per trip, so that we can bring the cost down as much as possible and maximize our time.

For this we will pick up a 26-footer with a lift-gate and do as many trips as we can with that truck in one day. At the time of this writing, we are set to have several pick-ups on Monday. In total we will grab about 36 pallets (3 trips) that day.

For us in this upcoming example, this works out to the following:

$90/day rental
$50/gas
$21.60/mileage
Total: $161.60

$161.60/36 gaylords = $4.49 per gaylord of added costs. $75+$4.49= **$79.49/gaylord**

**My two main sources are within city limits, so I have the advantage of spending less on mileage and gas for the most part.

Also, worth noting is that most suppliers deal with price per pound. This almost always works to your advantage as long as what you are getting are solely books.

If you buy gaylords with a vendor at a flat rate, that is also ok. What is NOT ok, is when they start to fill them up less and less over time.

If you start to see that, you should politely point that out, as it is part of the agreement to buy full gaylords of books – not half full!

When looking at other items such as buying a pallet jack or renting a storage unit, you should not be factoring those into your cost per gaylord.

That is because you are going to be consistently using these in theory for every load you pick up and process.

When trying to nail down any bulk sources in your area, you really should consider going to visit that particular place in person. Nothing is more important than visiting a source in person for the first time in order to put a face to your name.

Meeting someone in person is so underrated these days.

If you are nice, respectful, and approachable, you have a great shot at success. Who do you think the store owner/manager is ultimately going to give their business to – someone they met in person or someone over the phone?

I think we both know you have a much higher chance of earning the business if you show up in person ready to roll.

The best sources I have, I didn't call over the phone. I went to them in person. With all of them I was able to build a mutual trust and respect for each other. That is probably why I still have their business.

What you need to do first is get in touch with a Goodwill outlet. Most Goodwill locations across America operate under their own set of rules and regulations.

The person you are looking for is going to depend on what region you are in and how they like to operate.

Here are specific titles you are going to want to search for: warehouse supervisor, commodities sales manager, Post retail operations, or recycling manager.

There will also be other titles that are relevant, but these specific people will be in charge and are who you want to contact.

Find out where they operate out of (usually in the warehouse), and make it a point to meet them in person, especially if you are unable to get ahold of them via email.

A great tool to help you in your search of your decision-maker is going to be LinkedIn. I have used LinkedIn several times to find exactly who I was looking for, with great success.

Type in those same career titles I just gave you and add any additional filters needed such as outlet and location.

There is a reason I suggested going to Goodwill to start. It's good to get a baseline of pricing in your area for bulk books. From my experience, Goodwill seems to be priced low-medium on the spectrum in terms of price.

They are considered the low-hanging fruit and they happen to be all over the country. You most likely have a Goodwill outlet somewhat close to you.

Make sure you are buying their raw, unsorted product when you do establish them as a contact. <u>Their pre-sorted material is not worth your time.</u>

When I go to negotiate with other vendors, I am always able to bring up the fact that I buy decent product from Goodwill and get my pallets for .05 a lb.

Most vendors are charging much more than that if they have half-way decent product, so that lets them know that they need to work on their pricing if they want to work with us.

In fact, in this situation I often will mention what price I am use to paying before price is talked about. That's because I already know they are more expensive.

Don't Put the Cart Before the Horse

DO NOT try and get into a space prior to finding multiple bulk book sources and negotiating with them. That would be putting the cart before the horse (and you'll see why).

Imagine you love the idea of this business and you go out and find a small warehouse or storage unit to get started immediately on going bulk.

It seems logical right? You need a place to put all the 1000's of books you're going to buy! Wrong. Picture this, you find a place and you put down a security deposit, first month's rent, and get a lease term of 1-2 years.

You then go out all pumped up to go get vendors. You thrive under pressure, and figured this would light the fire inside you to go out and lock down sources.

Since you are now the proud new tenant of a warehouse or larger storage unit, you need to make sure that you start filling it up immediately!

Only thing is, after a week or two, you have called/dropped by every conceivable bookstore, thrift store, and donation-based company in your whole town and didn't get a single "yes" to start getting books. Or maybe no one has the number of books you need on a consistent basis. OOPS.

This HAS happened to people I know.

Do not let yourself get in a situation like this – you need to do all your homework first. You need to simultaneously be working on finding a suitable place and getting your sources lined up. It's a bit of a balancing act, but one that is totally manageable.

In order to circumvent this, all you need to do is come to an agreement on a date you intend of purchasing your first load of books (hopefully with more than one source as a fallback). At that point, it would be safe to look into moving into a spot. But ONLY then.

Always Act Larger Than You Are

This is another important aspect of getting into the bulk game. No one who deals with larger, consistent vendors on a regular basis wants to deal with a smaller "new guy" who has no idea what he is getting into.

Many vendors such as Goodwill have dealt with hundreds of small-time sellers that over promise and under deliver on just about anything you can think of.

Examples:

"We just want to start out small and do a test run, but next time we will do a full semi-truck load" (only to never make good on that since they are working out of mom's garage).

"Ya, I've been a long-time bulk book buyer. Oh, by the way, what size truck do I need to come pick up those 48 gaylord pallets?"

If you are going to act large initially, you'd better know what you are talking about beforehand. It's easy to spot someone who is new to this, especially if you are one of those vendors who sees this routine day in and day out.

What you need to do beforehand to act the part is to do your homework! You need to know all the lingo.

You need to understand the process and the timelines, Etc.

With most of these vendors you are only going to have one shot, so don't mess it up. Perfect practice makes perfect.

For several reasons I am going to list things you should know in terms of lingo, specs, etc:

Liftgate – Located on end of the truck for locations that do not have "dock wells" or "docks" to back your truck up to. Most warehouses that have these usually have steel ramps that can be manipulated to go up or down so they can accommodate a 16, 26, or 53 footer.

If you are doing a test run, you are going to be using a 16-footer or a 26 footer initially to test a small batch of books

You don't want to buy a 48'-53' footer worth of books, only to find out they are junk. If that was the case, you would be waving goodbye to $1,000's of dollars.

Truck sizes:

1. 16-footer: Can carry up to 6 gaylords total.
2. 26-footer: Can carry up to 12 gaylords total (unless it is CDL rated for much more weight. In that case, you can double-stack 24 gaylords total, as long as its rated for the weight).
3. Semi (53' Dry Van): 40-48 gaylords depending on who you use.

Pallet/gaylord combos: This is the term vendors use for charging additional for the pallet and box. These can be very expensive depending on where you buy. It's not uncommon to be charged anywhere from $15-$25 for the combo. If you are buying a semi-truck full that can really add up.

*Make sure to ask if they give you a credit when you supply them back to them each time.

Pallet Jack: Piece of equipment used to pull gaylords into the trucks. They will rarely ever drive a forklift into a 16 or 26-footer, so they will expect you to move them in once they have dropped them on the edge of the truck. You should always have one of these handy wherever you go.

More important factors in order to appear larger than you are will be the following:

Email Signature. This one can be a dead giveaway. Make sure your email signature looks professional. It should have the following information on your email sign off:

Hayden Aquilon
Company Name | www.companyname.com
Your address here.
512-295-xxxx
Company email here
WE. BUY. BOOKS. <<< (tagline here)

Company business cards. I have been guilty of this several times. I always run out and forget to restock my wallet. Make sure you always have these handy and ready to pass out.

When a new prospective vendor asks for your card to get ahold of you, it's usually so they can go back and do some research on you and potentially your website to see what kind of service/products you provide.

Website. If you don't have a website, you are not going to appear very credible. Period. That screams unprofessionalism. Get a decent website put together that at least has a contact form on it so people can reach you.

Together, all of this will help you to appear larger than you are and give off a much better impression of you and your business.

Endless Business Models

There is no one size fits all way to achieve success in this business. There are so many different ways to make money selling books and other media online/offline. I laugh at how obsessed people get with posting their Amazon sales graphs on Instagram and using it for screen savers.

I'll never forget one time when a fellow seller asked me how I had done in a previous month in terms of my sales (sales never matter by the way – it's all about profits). I quickly sent him over my sales chart and he replied by saying that he had finally beat me in sales over a month's time.

I snickered and said that while that may be true on Amazon, that only accounted for about 30% of my total current business revenue. I have multiple streams of income from media, most of which doesn't come from Amazon.

He was intrigued and wanted to learn more. People get so hung up with beating each other's Amazon seller app number that it is all they focus on.

There is no SINGLE way to make this model work.

In fact, if you are only utilizing one type of income stream then you are at a disadvantage. You need to spread your risk by having more than one income stream.

Here is a list of some of the many ways you can make money with this:

-List books on Amazon.com, ebay.com, abebooks.com, etc.
-Sell your "duds" to buyback companies.

-Sell lots on Facebook marketplace and Craigslist.
-Sell wholesale pallets to other sellers, thrift stores, etc.
-Wholesale "green" pallets to other Amazon sellers.
-Become a bulk book broker and take a % of sales.
-Consulting other book sellers/Starting a membership site, etc.
-Start your own used book store/run an online store simultaneously
-Sell your books at swap meets

The list goes on and on. The important part is that you optimize one of these types of income streams before you move onto others.

Right now, my favorite model is wholesaling books to other FBA sellers. It is such a clean model. We don't have to list. We don't have to worry about re-pricing.

We are able to completely streamline everything in terms of the scanning/sorting process and it allows me to scale up quickly, focusing on just a few components.

That is one of the reasons we were able to get into a larger warehouse this year. We didn't upgrade just once either, we upgraded twice!

You are essentially providing the pick axe during the proverbial digital "gold rush" (which it certainly is).

Others have tried wholesaling and hated it. It does come with its own types of headaches.

Namely, getting a large shipment of gaylords that are complete trash and unknowingly off-loading that to another seller who clearly isn't going to be happy.

Something like this can be a major roadblock to trust, re-ordering and a waste of resources.

In order to wholesale effectively, you need quite a bit of space. You also need to have a decent size list of clients that will buy from you, as well as access to trucks constantly (if you are doing the drop offs).

Let's break down several of these models so you can get a better idea of the inter-workings of each. That way you can find out what may be a good fit for you to pursue.

Selling Books Direct to Consumer Sites

As far as a long-term play, I believe this one tops the list as making the largest financial impact. At the end of the day, your goal should really be to take sales off of these large platforms that do not give you access to customers data.

That means selling off your own website, where you can collect customer data.

However, in the interim, selling on other platforms is ideal for immediate traffic and lots of cash. In the beginning, you have to play the game, and they get to make the rules.

As I have said before, you can start and scale this business very cheaply and safely. You don't need to over-leverage yourself or expand too fast.

In hindsight, I would have invested in a software that allows you to post simultaneously into several online book selling platforms. There are several out there.

What else these platforms do is make the listing, cataloging, and order fulfill process smooth as butter.

A few examples of these platforms are Cash Monkey and Netoscan. They cost up to 10x more than traditional software and require large set-up times.

*Update: It turns out that right before I was about to publish this book, my current listing software now has the new added capability to list on multiple platforms.

I decided to give this update to show you guys how nimble and fast changing the software team is over at Accelerlist. They are quickly adapting, and are always taking feedback seriously.

I am constantly told that I need to make the switch over to these larger services to really expand my business. What is ironic, is that some of these people are no longer in business and others are constantly jumping ship to different services.

current business model is perfectly suited for what we in place now. When the time comes that I feel it's ary, we will do what we have to.
es along with the same principle of maximizing your fore you upgrade. People get so caught up in and tweaking their systems. I'm all for that, but to have the sales first. Those same people are cart before the horse.

Wholesaling

This can be very situational in nature. Let me explain. It's not always a good idea to wholesale to others. There are so many situations where it can be to your benefit, but it can also come back to bite you.

Wholesaling can be smart to do when your cash-flow is out of whack, or if you're running out of room.

There are going to be times when you are strapped for cash.

There is no doubt about it. Sometimes you won't want to sell any of your pallets, especially if they are good ones. But there will be times when you don't have a choice.

If you have to get rid of your pallets, I recommend that you double the price you bought them for. If you have to deliver them locally, make sure you do it when you already have the truck booked for other reasons. You don't want to add an unnecessary expense. If they are a decent drive away, add on a delivery fee.

If you don't feel like driving, that's ok. Have them rent a truck and come pick them up on their own.

This next part people may find controversial, and that is fine.

In my opinion, it's just smart business. Let's say that right now, you have found yourself four sources. In general, some of these sources will be better than others. If you have a source that isn't as good as the others and your warehouse is full, it would serve you well to wholesale out your lowest yielding source to clients.

Let me be clear. I'm not saying sell them trash product. I'm saying get rid of your least profitable and make room for better yielding books. YOU have done all the work to find these. They are YOUR sources. Do with them what YOU please.

One more thing on this. There are pleasurable people to work with and miserable people to work with. Don't work with people who only seem to complain and whine. Get rid of them immediately. They aren't worth it.

I first heard this on a podcast several years ago and more recently from a family member who utilized this same thing in their medical practice. Once they got rid of their horrible clients, their lives got better immediately.

Go all in on your clients that are consistently good people. There are plenty of them out there – go find them ASAP.

Remember how I said wholesaling can come back to bite you? Well, here is an example.

Let's say you have been selling wholesale continuously to someone in your same town for quite some time. Business is good and the extra cash you get from them is a great added income stream for you.

You start to get greedy and keep giving them more and more product. They have gone from a storage unit to a warehouse and seem to be doing really well. Then one day it happens.

Why hasn't Jim called me recently? I hope he is doing ok. I'd better call him to see when he is coming by next. No answer.

You try two days later - no answer again.

The following week you go to reorder another truck load from your source. "Sorry Hayden, we just sold our load to another company we started working with, and he's paying us more".

Turns out it was Jim. OOPS!

Think very carefully before you start to wholesale to other people. You need to be strategic with how you proceed at all times.

There truly are millions upon millions of books out there for the taking, but if you guys are that close together with very limited supply, obviously interests can eventually collide.

Selling to Buyback Sites

No matter what your business model is, you have to sell your books & other media to as many buyback sites as possible to maximize your profits.

My company makes thousands of dollars per month from utilizing multiple buy back companies. This is what our sorting tables currently look like below. Notice how we have the three separate buyback site bins?

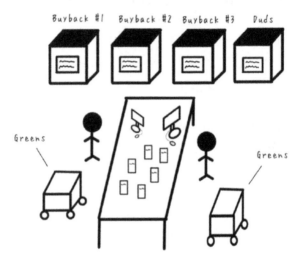

As you progress throughout your journey, you may find yourself switching business models to satisfy your ideal type of work day. Some people hate dealing with listing, some people hate fulfilling orders.

Do whatever type of model gets you the most excited to get out of bed each day and make the most of it.

For me personally, I don't enjoy listing and order fulfillment. So, I said to hell with it, and tried something new. We now get to focus our attention on just a few things and get to go all in on them.

Don't forget, the one factor that will always remain steady is sending in product to buy back sites. Spend a decent amount of time researching them and working with as many as you can.

When you finally do get into a warehouse, it doesn't matter what model you choose – you're going to need help. Chances are if you aren't getting help, you are not maximizing the efficiency of your space.

When Is It Time to Hire?

When it's time to hire, don't wait around to find someone. I put my first 1099 contractor in place the moment I could hire them, even though it took away from my take home pay.

What you want to do from the start is identify the most painful/hard aspect of running a book business. For you is it scanning that makes you miserable? Is it listing? Whatever the case may be, find someone to replace you so you can focus on what you enjoy, and then drive incremental revenue.

Your first couple hires will undoubtedly be 1099 contractors that are either listers or scanners for you.

When you do make your first couple hires, you need to take into consideration that your short-term performance goals you set for your business will be temporarily slowed down as you on-board and train new employees.

Initially, your business will suffer from productivity decline in the short-term, but should return much more productive than previously before once you have trained your employee(s).

This is due to taking yourself out of the productivity equation in the short-term. You will be training your employee as much as you can, until that person can be fully independent without you.

I would always make your first couple hires sorters/scanners. This is due to a low margin of error and not a ton of one-on-one training. This role is centered around using and relying on software 99% of the time.

If the certain individual you hired simply goes off the software triggers you have set and you clearly mark the different bins, there should be NO issues.

It will all simply become a matter of getting their reps in and becoming faster over time at scanning items.

If you are hiring someone as a lister, which I recommend later on, you will be involved in much more hands-on training, as there are plenty more aspects to look out for.

Make sure you get with your accountant regarding any questions geared towards hiring new employees. Make sure you can hire someone as an independent contractor versus a W2, etc.

You need to make sure you are following the labor laws so you don't get in trouble with the IRS.

For more information on making the right hiring distinction, I have listed the IRS site below that clearly defines this:

https://www.irs.gov/businesses/small-businesses-self-employed/independent-contractor-defined

If you are really wanting to accelerate growth, do not wait to make these lower-level hires for sorting and listing.

You must always be thinking and evaluating what is worth YOUR time, and knowing what is below your pay grade. If you are offering someone $10-$12/hour to sort books, that means that if you were to do it yourself, you are valuing your time at that same cost.

Isn't your time worth more than that? ...I would hope so.

What I did early on was figure out what I wanted my time to be worth in the beginning, and align my thinking and actions around that number.

That helped me set daily cherry-picking goals. It helped me understand how many stores I had to hit, how many books I needed to find, etc.

As you go along your journey, you will consistently need to rethink how to center this hourly value around your new activities, such as transitioning into bulk.

For most of you, your time will be spent managing people, making sales calls, renegotiating with vendors, etc.

When you are unable to assign a monetary value to something like finding new sources, you need to instead understand what you would pay someone else to be an outside sales rep, which will help you arrive at an hourly rate there. Any decent outside sales rep can make 80-100k a year, or more.

Your job as the captain of the ship should be to always go after sales and look for new revenue sources.

Below is an extensive list of priorities for your book business that you must focus on:

1. **Lead generation**. Setting up a clear way for people to contact you. Website → lead form/phone number. Don't just leave it up to a client to initiate contact. Make them able to be contacted as well. Collect their phone number or email address and get into communication with them ASAP. A short contact form is best for this. Go and check out my website for any ideas!
https://www.austinbookdonations.com
2. **List of Suppliers.** Building a long list of potential bulk book suppliers that you can draw from. Sources dry up or stop working with people all the time. You need to have a backup plan.
3. **Make sure you're covered**. It's not acceptable to cut corners without things like business insurance. Accidents happen ALL the time. Don't be cheap/procrastinate about getting proper coverage for your business just to save a few bucks. You'll regret it all later. Side Note: We've been in 3 separate accidents in rental trucks. Damaged our forklift and stacker. We have also damaged one of our warehouses. Luckily, we were covered.
4. **Find ways to monetize EVERYTHING.** One of the main issues with selling books is finding ways to get rid of your "duds". This is the 70% of the books you can't use. At the time of this writing, we go through a minimum of 40-48 gaylords a week. That's A LOT of duds. You have to find a place for them to

go efficiently and cheaply. Ideally you need to get paid for them. Currently we monetize every single book, unless it is badly damaged.

5. **Managing the Numbers.** You need to be tracking everything. Establish a standard for your listers and scanners. Hold them to reasonable numbers. At the end of the day you need a list of KPI's (Key performance indicators). These can include, but are not limited to:
   -Number of pallets scanned/day
   -Number of books listed/day
   -Number of contacted clients
   -Number of new sources called on
   ....etc.

Scaling Up

You need to realize that your time is limited – there are only so many hours in the day. At some point, you can't keep adding more hours onto your work day.

You need to think bigger in order to achieve your goals. It's going to take a team for most of you to get where you want to go. You can't do it alone.

Most of you reading this have a day job that you have to attend which is a 9-5.

Some of you drive for uber or do any of the flexible delivery options that are available to you.

Let me tell you right now, it's going to be substantially harder to go "full-time" when you are working a 9-5 versus a flexible schedule. Especially if you support a family and have high monthly cash obligations.

I believe what it comes down to is making that mental break through of going from having security to having no consistent paycheck. No matter what, you are going to have to come to terms with this at some point to make the actual "jump".

This stops a lot of people dead in their tracks. Right now, I have a friend who is the absolute model of a hustler. He HUSTLES. He has four kids, most of them young. He's married and he is on the road for his job several hours a day, yet he still sources every single second he can out of the day to try and get ahead.

He has been at it for years. When we talk (which is every day), he sounds like a broken record. "I hate my job, I hate this commute, I can't do this anymore".

The single most asked question he is always pondering with me is this: "How do I actually make the jump over to going full-time on this?"

We have talked about this in depth several times, but he hesitates on taking action because of the mental block of losing his salary and foundation for his family. How can you blame him!?

If I am being perfectly honest, I actually have told him not to make the jump over. That is because I know he is not in the right place mentally. He isn't ready. He knows exactly what needs to be done, but he won't go through with it. I do believe that if he was mentally prepared, he could make the jump today.

There are a few key components he is missing. The first is the **mindset**. The second are the **systems**. He doesn't have systems in place to run smoothly without him. The third thing is that he doesn't know his **numbers** well enough.

How can you know if you are ready to make the jump without knowing your numbers!?!

He also does not have a consistent supply of sources to draw from. Hustle ISN'T enough.

Below I ask him a couple questions that reaffirm he isn't on top of his numbers. It also shows he has no idea what he needs to do in order to make this a full-time thing!

Me: "Hey brother, how many units would you have to sell per day to go full-time (or basically replace your income) per day?

Him: **Crickets...**

Me: "Ok...well what is the average profit per unit that you sell?

Him: "I don't know, I would have to look at the numbers."

Me: "Well what would you say is a ball-park average."

Him: "Honestly, I have no idea off-hand."

Let me ask you guys something – does that sound like someone who is ready to make the jump over?

There is no goal set. There is no accountability. There is no clear road map. There is literally nothing.

So how can we help him? Let's turn this into a real-life example.

Let's say your average profit per book after all fees and expenses is $5 (This is average).

How many books would you need to replace a $50,000 salary? That is 10,000 books over the course of a year. You would have to sell 27 books per day. That is not very hard.

But that's not the whole story is it? What about your overhead? You'll most likely have a warehouse. You'll have to have someone hired to scan and list for you.

Warehouse - $1,200/month x 12 = $14,400
Full-time Hire - $1,920/month = $24,480

There's another $38,880. Now all the sudden you need to sell 17,776 books over a year. That is 49 books per day. Still completely doable.

Yes, there are some other expenses here and there. But I also, lowered the average profit for this example. My point is that now you can see a much clearer picture of what it takes to achieve your goal.

It's clear – down to the exact book. This is exactly how I got to where I am. It's what kept me sane and kept me going with confidence.

If you are currently at this full-time, then what is keeping you from scaling up? If you know your numbers and have a complete handle on your business, you should be trying to scale up as fast and SAFE as possible.

This month alone, I have added a full-time employee and another part-time employee. I have worked out the math and know how profitable every employee I add is to me.

I also have a benchmark so I know what is expected when I add in another employee. If you start to bring on more help, but the production of each additional person isn't proportional, something is wrong.

Beforehand, I didn't know the answer to that question so I had to go and find out for myself. Software has helped me tremendously with this.

If you are having trouble scaling profitably and are running into cash flow issues, you need to seek money cheaply. Ideally, this will be other people's money whenever you can.

You see, there is income and there is cash flow. A business that can't sustain the necessary level of cash flow is a business that is being held back from growing.

Even if you are profitable, you may have a lag on your income collection. Examples could be Amazon's two-week payout holding you back, or accounts payable that have not been collected from several of your buyback vendors or clients you wholesale to that have net 10-30 terms.

This is precisely why I hold onto debt and strategically utilize it whenever possible. It's important to be sitting on a lot of cash at all times. CASH IS KING. I am ok with paying interest because I know the return is much higher redeploying the cash.

Let's use a recent example to explain this. Let's say you have a credit card that has a $5,000 limit on it. You haven't put any purchases on it because you are worried you won't be able to pay it off in full and hate paying interest.

You've been scaling fast and buying lots of product. You have been paying for everything with your debit card and pride yourself on having no debt.

Suddenly you realize that it is Oct 30 and your rent is due in 2 days. But you won't be getting your Amazon payout for another week. Your upcoming payout is $12,000, but that doesn't really matter in this scenario, does it? OOPS.

Oh my, you also have an employee to pay for their last two weeks of work. Do you think they accept credit card payment? Lol, nope.

You need to get comfortable with holding debt if you want to grow and scale. You need to hold onto cash for important payments for things like rent/lease and employee pay.

Again, in this example the business IS profitable and making profits but they lack the cash flow! Without it, they are in major trouble.

You can't go without paying rent and you can't stiff your employees on their pay or you simply won't have a business.

With all that said, let me tell you what is NOT ok in this scenario. You have to always be looking at your business health on a daily basis. I have a spreadsheet I update daily at the end of the day. I don't want something automated. I NEED to see this daily. It serves as a reminder. It keeps me in "the know".

Software like QuickBooks also has a few days lag on it, plus your accountant will almost never update this daily for you. They tend to update it in blocks around the end of the month.

If you are operating with debt and your debt is outweighing your net cash, you are headed in the wrong direction and are certainly going to be in trouble.

For example, if you have a credit card with $10,000 on it and you have $2,000 in the bank with a $3,000 Amazon payment coming, you have a net deficit of $5,000 in cash. Not an ok situation.

On the other hand, if you owe $10,000 on a credit card, have 2,000 in the bank and 8,000 in cash coming from Amazon, that is a much better situation. Net 0 cash in my opinion is also totally fine, but not long-term.

For months I operated like that, but I also was paid a salary out of that. That's another large distinction.

Pro Tip: Find potential access to money early on – I.E Line of credit, loan, or investments from friends or family. Keep them informed throughout your journey by sharing your progress. When you do finally need the cash, they will be much more inclined to fork it over.

Your Work Space

So, you have a space now - congrats. How should it be set up? What type of layout is ideal? What are additional considerations for the area you should pick? What type of equipment is essential to start out?

Don't worry, we'll get into those questions right now.

The answer to many of these questions is all going to depend on how big of a business you are looking to build. What are your financial goals? Do you want the headache of dealing with employees?

Let's set the stage by giving you a peek into my business as a whole, so we have a place to start from. It will give you a good idea of what you need to do to make your business a reality.

As I write this book, I have a 4,400 square foot with another 600 square feet of air-conditioned office. This amount of space gives you the options to pursue basically any business model that you would like to.

As I mentioned before, we are mostly on the wholesale business side these days, but we are also set up to sell DVDs, CDs, and books direct to consumers through our own fulfillment as well. We also have several thousand books that sit at Amazon's warehouse.

On our own shelves, we basically put any books that are ranked 2 million or higher that we don't send to our clients.

The type of business model that you are looking to pursue is going to be directly tied into how large of a warehouse you choose.

Larger Warehouse Spaces

3,000 SQFT +
Ideal for sellers who plan to do Merchant fulfilled or a hybrid of MF and wholesale.
-You need room to set up adequate shelving.
-Store full truckloads of pallets.
-Build and store sets and lots.
-Area for scanning and listing.
-Storage for buyback company pallets.
-Room to build Amazon FBA pallets.

Smaller Warehouse Spaces

3,000 SQFT or smaller
Ideal for strictly Amazon FBA sellers & wholesalers
-Room for full truckloads.
-Room to scan and process these loads (I.E. Sorting table).
-Listing stations.
-Area to build your Amazon FBA pallets.
-Room to store duds.

****You could argue that you should have a larger warehouse if you were strictly a wholesaler so that you could handle more volume, but the reality is that product should be leaving the warehouse as fast as its coming in.

P.S. For over a year, I was working out of a 1,000 Sqft warehouse doing amazon FBA and wholesaling. It sure wasn't roomy, but we made it work. I don't recommend it.

As you can see, I didn't get into where to set up everything up in detail. This book is centered around higher-level aspects of running the business.

There are literally THOUSANDS of YouTube videos that will not only explain that, but show you visually. All the nitty gritty details of setting up an account, listing, sorting, and organizing is all out there within a click of a button.

Setting Micro Goals

This is one of the most important parts of the book so please pay careful attention here. By the way, I hope you have been marking up your book with notes and highlights (it's the best way to retain information).

If you don't know what your goal is for this business, how can you know what you need to do in order to attain it?

Saying that you want to quit your job is very vague as a goal.

Think in terms of income. You need to assess what it is going to take to get to where you want to go.

Unlike many other books where they promise you'll make millions if you let go of your limiting beliefs and "grind it out," I am going to level with you and tell you that you'll be lucky to take home $30,000-$40,000 your first year.

If I just lost you right there, or you are wondering WTF Hayden? Take a deep breathe. Here is a reality check, followed by some good news.

You are starting your own business! You are reinvesting in things like equipment to get up and running. The fact you are even able to turn a profit is amazing in itself. This business has a ton of front-loading of capital if you want to scale quickly, which is pretty standard for any business type.

If you have ever started a business prior, you will know this. If you are coming from a cushy corporate job making six figures like I did, you're going to have to come to terms if you want to escape your 9-5.

You will take an income hit, period.

Now, let me give you the good news. End of year two is when you will start to "hit your stride" and be able to pay yourself more, should you choose to.

Your income will substantially increase by the end of year two. If you can't stay focused and dedicated to give something two years, you're NEVER going to make it on your own. EVER.

In order to hit the first-year numbers, let me make this tangible for you. Below, I have provided you with a road map of how you can get to the numbers I talked about.

There are a few assumptions that need to be made for this graph, as well as certain promises you need to keep to yourself to see these numbers to completion.

The first assumption is that you are shipping all your books LTL (which you need to). There is absolutely no reason not to. The excuse that you are scared and not sure how to, does not fly. There are several of these videos also on YouTube. Just type in, "how to ship an LTL pallet of books via Amazon FBA."

The second, is that you are going to be shipping an average of 750 books out per week. Trust me when I say, that is nothing. That should be easy for you to do. Basically, each month a total of three pallets will go out (about 3,000 books).

The other metrics are straight forward and for the most part, inflated so that there is margin for error. For example, I put LTL inbound at .12 a lb. I get between .06-.10 usually.

Average buy cost per book is at $1.50, I am at $0.44 cents a book. Average sale price is $12.50. My overall historical is $12.91.

As you can see, everything set below is completely reasonable, so you should be able to beat all these metrics below.

0	750	$1.50
Starting Inventory	Books Listed Per Week	Average Buy Cost
$0.12	5.0%	$12.50
Inbound Shipping Per Book	Turn Rate Per Week	Average Sales Price

So, what is the best way to go about this?

This is a great time to share the journey of one of the guys I mentor named Cody. Cody has been at this just about a year or so, and has done things similar to my path.

He started small and used his cash flow to reinvest over and over again. He now is in a warehouse and has an employee working alongside him and his wife.

He is also on his way to opening up his own bookstore that is part of the warehouse that he already operates in, which is very smart.

That will allow him to add sales of product he may not be able to monetize as easily, and to do so with almost no additional overhead in terms of rent cost.

I share this with you to show you how quickly you can gain momentum in this business. He and I spoke not long ago over the phone about his goals for 2021.

I pointed out how if he changed nothing and did the same volume as he is doing now, he will easily surpass $500,000 next year without working any harder. The first six months of 2020, he was hardly putting up any numbers.

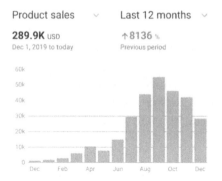

Instagram - @cody.estes

I can't wait to see what becomes of his business in the future. His journey is not uncommon either. There are plenty of people doing it!

Remember, it's best to start small – maximizing the space you have. If you have your sights set on big numbers, you will be able to smoothly transition into larger spaces to accommodate your volume. Don't bite off more than you can chew. <u>Don't rush yourself</u>.

If you would be thrilled to have a business that eventually does about a $1,000,000 a year in sales and puts a minimum of 20% of that in your pocket, then you certainly don't need more than 4,000-5,000 sqft.

If you want to do bulk media but don't need to sell a million a year to hit your goals, you can have a much smaller work space.

If you are just wanting to do this as a side hustle to generate an extra $1,000-$2,000 a month, that is going to be easy.

Find out what the exact amount is that you want to achieve and go from there.

Just remember, warehouses don't get much smaller than 1,000 sqft. At that point you will be looking at a storage unit or some type of flex-space building.

If you are looking at doing something smaller than 1,000 sqft, you should really aim to work out of your garage if you have one. I know several people who have done this to get started.

If you go the storage unit route, here are issues you can face with storage units in addition to limited space:

-Hours of access that are limited.
-Potential access points that are a pain in the butt to maneuver with large trucks.
-No access to power within the unit.
-No adequate lighting.
-Raised asphalt "lip" on the unit so that water does not enter space (makes it very hard to roll over).
-No dock well for truck to back into.
-No wifi accesss.

As you can see, there are several road blocks to consider but there is a trade off with what you have to pay monthly to utilize storage unit space.

People make this work all the time. I know a handful of people that are currently making this happen.

Worth adding - you would be very surprised to find how cheaply you can get into warehouse space depending on what part of the US you live in. I was recently speaking at an event

I highly recommend for all booksellers called "Turn the page".

I was surrounded by a couple of successful bulk book buyers who were all paying incredibly cheap rent for their spaces, as their warehouses were in places like Indiana, Alabama, and Connecticut. There was even a gentleman there that was only paying $2,000 a month in San Diego, CA for 2,500 sqft.

Point being, don't write off getting a smaller warehouse if you can find a sweet deal on one. My friend found a 2,500 sqft warehouse for $750 a month in Alabama. That is ridiculously cheap.

The ideal situation to get started and test the waters is going to be in your own home garage – cleaned out of course!

That is how I, and many others have started. No additional overhead needed. You are already paying for the roof over your head, the wifi, and the utilities you will be using.

There are even additional tax advantages such as a home office exemption, but that is something you must talk to your accountant about.

Take Immediate Action.

Do NOT wait to take action on everything you are learning in this book. Selling books on Amazon is such a great starting point to enter into the online sales world, no matter what direction you want to end up heading.

Start sourcing books immediately. Download a scouting app, get the free trial and get a blue tooth scanner such as the Eyoyo and get rolling!

Within a two-days you can get your equipment in the mail and go out and start grabbing books. You could have your first sale the day you go out too. It all depends on if you sell it fulfilled by Merchant (FBM), or you send it Fulfilled by Amazon (FBA).

FBA has a much longer turn around, but you can also fetch a premium on the item's sale price.

The best part is this: If you end up hating sourcing books or it just isn't right for you and your schedule, you can call it quits with literally little to no money spent at all.

Heck, you can even resell your Bluetooth scanner on Amazon or eBay. This is one of the few business that hardly requires ANY overhead to get started.

Find Accountability Partners Doing the Same Thing

Have you ever been to a gym and seen a trainer that was working with someone one on one? Ever notice how some of them don't seem to be in shape, yet their whole job is to show people how to be?

For the longest time I would always wonder why someone would choose to work with a trainer who was not physically fit themselves. Seems like a logical assumption, right?

Here is the reality. It doesn't matter if the trainer is fit or not if the accountability is there.

You see, most people don't need to be shown what to do. They know how to do the exercises. They already may be fit, or are on their way to becoming fit.

The trainer's main job is to simply keep these people accountable for their actions. They make sure they show up to class, and that while they are there, they give it their all.

That is precisely the reason you need to find an accountability partner. Make sure that you find someone as motivated as you are before you commit to working together. You want someone who is going to push you further, call you out on your laziness, and constantly motivate you.

You will want to set up calls with these people each week to check in and go over your wins and losses.

Talk about what is working in your business and see how you guys can help each other whenever possible.

I can't tell you how valuable these calls have been for me. Never discount having an accountability partner who is more behind in their journey than you are.

Often times they can come with the best insight and ideas because they have a fresh perspective.

If you don't have an accountability partner yet, go out and get one ASAP. It does not matter what part of your journey you are in. The earlier, the better.

PART FIVE: TOOLS TO PUT IN YOUR TOOLBOX

Mindset

Recently my dad got started selling books online due to me constantly harassing him on a daily basis.

Being a new seller, he obviously had tons of questions in the beginning, many of which probably seemed daunting to him at the start.

What is interesting to me is that his main question was how I personally got my mindset to do this on a continuous basis, and how I am able to keep growing in terms of sales.

It's a great question, and one that I certainly know the answers to. There is a mix of several things it boils down to.

I treat all of this like a treasure hunt (because it actually feels that way to me - I love what I do). That keeps me excited and motivated to get moving every day. Every single day is different!

I am obsessed with books. I get to be around books all day long – hundreds of thousands of them at any point in time.

Imagine if you were a dog-lover and got to run a dog kennel with thousands of dogs every day, you'd probably be a pretty happy camper!

I love to win and I am also a sore loser, which makes me try even harder. Whenever I would cherry pick (which I still do on occasion) I was always first anywhere I went. That meant being up extra early, mapping out places effectively, and sticking to the plan. Being **first** matters, so don't slack off and think it's okay to arrive places after they've been picked through.

I always ask questions everywhere I go. The stupid questions, the uncomfortable questions, the hard questions. These have made me great contacts, made for great negotiations, and have opened up many doors for me.

There is a darker motivation for me here as well. It's the fear of failing and having to go back to work at a "real job".

That is always in the back of my mind. It's a fear that keeps the fire inside me burning 24/7. It really is that painful of a thought for me.

They say that pain/fear are one of the major motivators, and they're right.

I can't think of anything worse than having to work for someone else. I believe it's even more true than ever now. Everything is so politically correct, structured, and corporate.

I still have many friends working in sales jobs that are absolutely miserable. Some make good money, some do not, but both are equally as unhappy at the end of the day.

One of my good buddies is still in his sales job, working to build his Amazon business so that he can quit (which he is close to doing).

Every time we talk, he agonizes about how bad his day-to-day is, how desperate he is to quit, and how lucky I am to have "made it to the other side".

I sympathize with him and try to keep him motivated, helping however I can.

Last, but not least, there is the monetary payoff that I love. I love knowing that at any point I am in complete control over the direction and profitability of my company.

In my mind, I know I am in complete control of my future and my income. At any point, I can figure out how to "give myself a raise" or to take my foot off the accelerator and take time for myself & my family.

In summary, the four main components that have helped shape my mindset boil down to these.

1. Obsessed with the product.
2. Ultimate will to win.
3. Fear of failure → back to 9-5.
4. Control over paycheck.

Hardware

Equipment, just like people, come in all shapes and sizes and are not all made equal - despite what some people would have you believe. Luckily for you, through trial and error I was able to weed out all the nonsense and provide everyone with a list of products (both software & hardware) that, in my opinion are the best out there.

I'm a big value guy, and I prefer to get the most bang for my buck. Yes, there is some hardware that may be a little bit nicer than what I have, but not at a price tag 4x-5x more than mine, so you can forget it.

To this day I still can't believe how inexpensive it is to get fully set up and rolling in this book business in the beginning. I sat down and tried to think of other business models that were as cheap to start and where you could start seeing an ROI as early as month two or three. It is simply incredible.

There is just a short list of items you need to get started. The most time-consuming part is setting up a professional Amazon seller central account, which can be done at www.sellercentral.amazon.com.

Since I am all about simplicity and maximizing my time - I am going to give you these resources in list form below.

There are about a million videos on all of these items out there on YouTube. I am not going to go into any specifics. It's all out there for you to easily access at the touch of a button.

1. Set up a seller central account.
2. Download ScoutIQ (scanning app).
3. Sign up for an account on Accelerlist (listing software).
4. Buy an Eyoyo scanner off of Amazon.
5. Buy both label printers (Zebra).
5. Buy Printer labels (Dymo).

Equipment
-Zebra LP 2844 - $90-$100 (To label boxes).
-Zebra LP 2824 - $40-$125 (to label books).
-Dymo Labels - $4-$6 a roll (1,000 per roll).
-Taotronics Scanner - $34.99 (Scan in books).

*This is all you need to get started. As your business grows and evolves, you will upgrade equipment and look for more expensive solutions that fits your needs. For now, you don't need anything more than this!

Software

The software aspect of this business is certainly worth mentioning, so we'd better cover it in depth here over the next several paragraphs or so. Do NOT skip over this part, as it will make you a ton of extra money if you try and implement what I cover.

In terms of software, you are going to have several different pieces that will come together to create a seamless, money-making machine.

You will be dealing with the following:

-Scanning software.
-Listing software.

-Repricing software.

Disclaimer: Depending on how you are running your business, how long you've been in business, and how large your business is from a revenue generating stand point, there are going to be lots of changes in what software and even hardware you use.

I am going to be covering the best early-to-mid range software to use since most everyone reading this will be in that vicinity.

With that being said, I will also point you in the right direction for people who are looking to get to that next level as well.

In terms of scanning software, there are two leading apps out on the market right now that are both reasonably priced.

The first one is called ASellerTool (Scoutly). This app costs about $20 a month and allows you to use it for either cherry picking or bulk.

The second is ScoutIQ (scoutiq.co), which I have used since day one for the most part. It costs just a tad more, but the interface is superior to Scoutly in my opinion.

Honestly, scoutIQ is basically the apple of computers and cell phones. It's design and simplicity are what take the cake. As we all know, people will pay more for features like that. That's what has made Apple so successful.

Another added bonus is that scoutIQ is smaller and nimbler, which seems to allow them to make needed changes to the app when they get feedback from their clients (which is on a continual basis).

They are very receptive to beneficial upgrades to the app, and have made several changes to the app for as long as I have had it. There is a private Facebook page for app users for trouble shooting, help, community, etc.

What both of these apps allow you to do is set your own "triggers," which determine what books go green for you that are considered acceptable to sell.

You can also add as many users on to these apps as you want to. Each additional user you add costs less each time. What is also a nice added touch is that you can enable the app to hide the prices of the books your employees are scanning so all they see are the specified colors for accept or reject.

The theory is that it potentially cuts down on someone wanting to take home the expensive books for themselves!

Until you are running your own merchant ful-filled operation where you have the space to hold onto books in your own inventory, do not mess with the default triggers that the app comes with.

Overall, the team over there have made tweaks to these triggers and they are set up to give FBA book sellers a great chance of success, by just using the default triggers.

One of my larger mistakes in this business was getting more lenient on what was to be acceptable for my app to flash green on certain books.

I continued to push back on the rank of the book, allowing slower selling books to go acceptable and taking books that weren't as profitable as they should be.

If you start to do this, you aren't going to see the ramifications until months later. This is due to long-term storage fees catching up to you and removal fees from these "long-tail" books.

As I mentioned before, long-tail books are books that take much longer to sell because the ranks are higher.

In my humble opinion, anything you send to FBA should be at least 2 million rank or lower.

There is one more feature you need to be aware of when you are looking at rank and sell-through rate, and that is what is called an escore.

Sometimes the rank of a book can be mis-leading since there can be sales spikes on a book or anomalies. As you get into the high X00,000+ ranked books, a single sale can really alter the rank of a book overnight.

This is when the escore comes into play. The escore is a number indicator that actually shows you how many books have sold over the course of a 6-month period. With this information handy, you can make a much better decision when selecting a book to keep.

As you can see in this example, this particular book is a high selling book. Not only is the rank low, but the escore is a 151+ (indicating that at a bare minimum, over 151 copies of this book have sold in recent months – this title in particular is probably selling thousands).

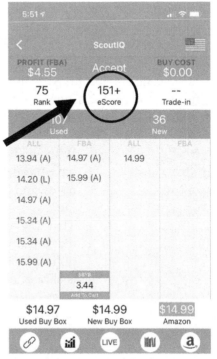

2,000,000 rank is my absolute ceiling for FBA. In addition, I like to see an escore around 5 or higher. When you go to price these types of books, I like to get a lot more aggressive with pricing so I can be one of the few to sell that particular title.

Just remember, the more books you take toward that end of the spectrum, the less sales you will likely encounter.

When it comes to listing software, Accelerlist is the program you are going to use to effectively list your books as cheaply and fast as possible.

When I first started out, I was resistant to investing in this software because I thought I was great at simply listing all these books on Amazon.com through their interface.

Had a known better, I could have been doing it 10x faster with a third-party software. That is when I eventually stumbled upon Accelerlist (accelerlist.com).

What is amazing about third party listing software is that you can <u>almost</u> automate the listing process. Basically, you can get it as stream-lined as possible.

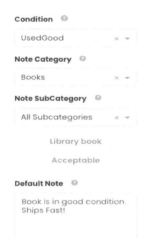

When you go to scan in a book, I have pre-designated condition, notes, and prices on my books.

That way when it is scanned in, all that information automatically populates into the fields. All I do is click one single button to process the book through. It literally takes just seconds.

As you can see in the picture above, all that data that I have pre-selected goes right into the listing itself, so I do not have to do any additional work to set up a listing.

You NEVER want to touch a book more than twice in total. The first time is when you initially scan it in with scanning software and then place in a certain conditioned pile.

The second is when you grab it from that pile to list it. I have heard of people that touch books several times throughout the whole process just to save a couple bucks here and there.

I value my time more than anything, so that is how I run my business.

You need to have an efficient processing table. You'll want tables that are labeled for your condition notes ahead of time so you know exactly where to put them.

Also, buy bins with rollers on the bottom of them. These are where you will put all your "green" (profitable) books.

Make sure they are stacked neatly. Not only will it maximize space, but it will keep them from getting damaged.

Ideally everything in your garage, storage unit, or warehouse is going to be mobile. You want to save your back and knees at all costs. This business can take a toll on you if you are not handling product the right way all the time.

I still cringe to this day when I see people not bending down and using their legs to pick up heavy boxes, constantly stressing out their backs. Mark my words, it will eventually catch up to you in this business if you aren't careful.

Here is the summarized list of all the software I use with associated cost:

-$44 ScoutIQ (scouting app).
-$34 Accelerlist (web-based listing software).
-$16 Repriceit.com (repricer for Amazon).
-$40 professional seller account.

That comes out to a $135 total monthly commitment. Again, look at how low the investment is. If you were to find just 20 books a month, you pay that off. We find that amount in 15 minutes or less these days.

> Pro-Tip: If you visit any YouTube video of mine, I have provided the direct links to all of these products in all my videos (it would be much easier to go through those links to ensure you are picking up the right equipment!).

In the next segment, I have a little present for you guys to get you started on finding sources and getting hooked up with buyback companies.

Bookmark Tab

I am going to give you guys some of the items I have on my bookmarks tab. Many of these are the exact book source links that I use that allow me to locate and buy hundreds of thousands of books.

At this point you need to go grab your laptop and add the following bookmarks:

Sellbackyourbook.com (buyback site)
Thriftbooks.com (buyback site)
Bookscouter.com (buyback site)
Abebooks.com (buyback site)
Discoverybooks.com (buyback site)
bstocksupply.com (liquidation site)
publicsurplus.com (liquidation site)
liquidation.com (liquidation site)
govdeals.com (liquidation site)
Craigslist.com (Book Supply + sales)
Restrictedinventory.com (Buyback site)
Facebookmarketplace.com (Book Supply + sales)

Buybackexpress.com (Buyback site)
Hpb.com (They have 120 stores nationwide. In person buybacks).

This should easily get you started. I have dozens more, most of them local to me. As you go through your journey you will end up with a large list like me with local buyers.

This leads us to the importance of building a network and relationships with buyers and sellers. It's something you can't overlook.

Importance of Networking

I often remember going out sourcing and running into many different resellers cherry-picking along the way. It's funny how secretive 99% of people are that are in this business.

They would do things like look over their shoulder constantly like they are shop lifting, or pretend to be reading a book when someone such as an employee would walk by.

That is just plain silly. Do NOT operate like this, EVER. Let it be known what you're up to. Talk to the employees, let them know what you do! Nine times out of ten if you make friends with them, they will help you in more ways than one!

If you see other people scanning, get to know them. Heck, even trade some sources with each other. Go to library sales together, meet ups, etc.

This is something I did with a few guys I know. It only made me that much more successful finding product.

I can't tell you how many great connections you can get by opening up to people about what you are up to. I have gotten several consignment deals, book leads, and mentors from that act alone.

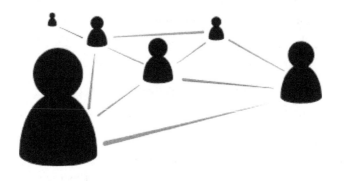

Another big one is connecting with people on social media. As mentioned previously, I have my own YouTube channel @haydenaquilon, where I constantly connect, network, and build relationships with all my followers who want to engage.

I continuously try my best to provide educational value to everyone that is curious and driven enough to figure out how to make money selling any type of media.

I give you everything you need to know to get started and thrive as you grow. Heck, I even reveal some of my bulk sources there.

At a recent event, a fellow bookseller named Avery alluded to how networking completely accounted for his success and how it is the number one thing that was his "tipping point".

By religiously posting on both YouTube and Instagram for a decent amount of time and also leveraging other people's audiences to grow his own, he was able to amass a decent-sized, hyper focused audience of "raving fans" in our niche.

From there he started a business selling other friend's and family's books, which quickly evolved to him selling many of his audiences restricted textbooks, since they are mostly gated.

"Gated" means that they are not able to sell those particular books on Amazon. Unlike some lucky individuals, they were not grandfathered in at an earlier time. In general, most "gated" books are textbooks which happen to be the most profitable.

If you happen to be out scanning and find high dollar value books that are restricted for you to sell (your app will tell you), do not leave them on the shelve, instead send them into restrictedinventory.com and you can still monetize it!

His last month sales (at time of writing of course) – amounted to over $70,000. Mostly all books he gets are for free, and he splits the profits 50/50 for whatever sells.

That is the power of networking. You can find him @romertheroamer on YouTube and Instagram.

For my own business, networking has done wonders for me. I have been able to collaborate with other local bulk book sellers in my state and strategically share sources with them.

I have also had the opportunity on several occasions to sell raw pallets of books to other smaller book sellers for a slight mark up on a continual basis.

You will find that this helps a TON with your cash flow. When you are a bulk bookseller you typically have thousands of dollars tied up in inventory at any given time.

Sharing my journey on my Instagram and YouTube accounts has consistently provided thousands of dollars in business opportunities for me in the form of mentorships, sources, coaching, strategic partnerships, and product promotion.

Let me ask you something? Can you really afford not to network?

Next, let me lead you to some great introductions to people that you can learn from and get pointed in the right direction.

Influencers to Follow

Along with networking comes following and learning from people who have accomplished what you are trying to achieve. These guys have surely made every mistake in the book and have learned from them all.

They now have paved the way for you to be successful. Pull out your phone and make sure you are following their social media accounts.

Steve Raiken
IG - @raikenprofit
Youtube – Raiken Profit

Raiken profit has been awhile for quite some time. He is a jack-of-all trades seller, as he has dabbled in just about everything online. He has great content for anyone interested in learning about library sales, estate sales, and hitting your local department stores such as Goodwill and Savers. He has a very large following on YouTube and I highly recommend following his inspirational content along with the additional gentlemen mentioned below.

David Chung
IG - @davecanread

David is a true OG in the book world. I first met David in Austin, TX at the "Turn the Page" event. What stood out to me is how humble and sincere he is. He has done tens of millions of dollars selling media and has been at it for over a decade.

If I ever need guidance, I call him first.

Christian/Adam -Latin Pickers
IG - @latinpickers
Youtube – Latin Pickers

These guys are some of my favorite to watch. They have had an amazing journey that started out using their home as their library and place to sort.

At this point in their journey, they now have two different warehouses and both live full-time off of their income. They sure seem to love what they do as well.

Make sure that if bulk is the road you want to go down, you check these guys out.

Reezy Resells
IG - @Reezyresells
YouTube – Reezy Resells

Reezy has been selling for quite a long time now and has amassed a sizeable following on both YouTube and Instagram. He has done about $5,000,000 in sales since he started.

His content was one of the first things I stumbled on when searching for bookselling related videos on YouTube. He now sells in several different categories these days.

Marek Konopka
IG - @polishhustler

These days Marek only deals with DVD's and CD's, but he used to be in the book business. I don't know anyone doing as much volume as he does with so little staff.

As of this writing, it is just him and three employees. Last I heard he had sold over 180,000 CD's so far in 2020, and that was as of November. That's a ton of CD's.

Caleb Roth:
IG - @thebookflipper
Youtube – Thebookflipper

Caleb has been an instrumental part of the book game. He is the creator of scoutIQ (scanning app) and eflip(OA – bookflipping online) as well as a minority owner in Accelerlist (listing software).

To this day, I still use his software for my bulk operation. His channel is ideal for individuals that are beginning/intermediate.

There is a great piece that he talks about all the time called "The hundred book challenge". Get over and watch that on YouTube if you are new to the game.

It is a great starting point. He is also the numbers guy. He covers several key metrics that you need to be aware of in order to run a healthy book business.
If you end up going the consignment route, I highly recommend that you get your hands on his bookselling spreadsheet.

In addition, for you bulk sellers, you can easily track what number of sales are coming from what sources. Obviously, this is highly valuable information to have access to.

The spreadsheet is priced very reasonably, and is a one-time purchase.

You can find it here:
https://www.thebookflipper.com/tracking-spreadsheet

Hayden Aquilon (Yours Truly)
IG: @haydenaquilonbooks
YouTube: Hayden Aquilon

Right below, you can instantly access my private group of hundreds of book sellers through the links provided if you have an eBook. For print and audio, you may have to work a tad harder by typing in the domain name ☺. You can also simply search "Hayden Aquilon books" under FB groups.

In addition, you can subscribe to my channel for plenty of additional value.

Trust….But Verify

Honestly, I don't know what is up with most people these days. It seems to me like people would rather act the part of success than actually becoming successful.

Everywhere I turn it's a constant post of an Amazon sales app screenshot that identifies absolutely nothing of meaning. Yet for them, it is a sign of pride and the hustle.

Naturally people who are not yet into this journey see things from the outside and gravitate towards these individuals with nice looking numbers.

Many of these guys are quick to offer up advice and usually just do so on their social media posts day in and day out. Some of it is wrong information or completely made up.

Most of the time, it may just be plain innocent hype and exaggeration. Point being, you need to be able to discern from what is real and what is completely made up.

This is not being said to simply call out the nonsense happening out there, but is a legitimate warning to all reading.

Many people may be basing their entire business plan/goals off of what is put out there on social media.

They may be risking a lot in order to take a dive into this business. When they finally get to the level which they think is going to be ideal for their goals or financial situation, they will be shocked/disappointed and possibly put in a compromised situation because they were mis-lead.

I can tell you right now, that as a general rule of thumb anyone doing less than around 20,000 a month in sales is not taking home much, if any.

Obviously, there are some additional things that need to be taken into consideration when I say this number. I mostly mean a bulk seller that has all the associated overhead.

If you are cherry-picking, it's going to be hard to ever hit this number consistently, but if you can, you will be making a nice chunk of cash in general if you buy right.

Most of you won't ever be able to hit that unless you have access to large amounts of sources in town, or have set up a lead generation source, such as a website.

If you consistently do library sales, estate sale clean outs, and larger commercial liquidations where you can grab lots of books then it is attainable.

I have found that the quickest way to "spot" if someone is serious about this or not is that they always know their numbers.

Also 99% of the time, they have an accountant or a bookkeeper that actually handles the books.

Last but not least, they pay themselves a salary. THAT is the key right there. If someone makes enough to pay themselves a consistent, pre-determined salary then they are reputable.

People who aren't doing this and putting up sales app screenshots that are low numbers are not only making NOTHING – most of them are actually continually feeding their business with their own money.

They seem to be completely oblivious to this because they don't know their numbers.

I want you all to succeed at this. And yes, I am talking to everyone putting up their sale app numbers I mentioned above as well. Let's have our particular industry be a leading example for transparency and what is actually achievable.

All I ask is that if you find someone out there that you enjoy following and maybe becomes your mentor, make sure you check off all the boxes.

I'm not asking you to be rude and ask them how much they make a year (they should not, and have no reason to tell you).

What I am saying is that you can indirectly ask questions around the topics stated above as if you are wanting advice.

For example:

When should I consider getting an accountant? At what point did you get one?

When did you start taking a salary, if any?

At what point in your journey were you able to take your business fulltime?

Ask these questions to get a read on them. We're not here to flush out charlatans, we are in this to make money. If you spotted a fake, move on and find someone else reputable to take advice from. No big deal.

Remember, Trust...but verify.

PART SIX: KNOW YOUR NUMBERS

Numbers are everything in business – put simply, if you aren't tracking numbers you are most likely running a half-ass operation. Numbers allow you to make smart, important decisions at a moment's notice. They allow you to see where you need to scale, where to trim the fat, and illustrate the overall health of your business.

As is true in other types of businesses, there are certain numbers that are key indicators of how you are doing as a whole.

In the case of books, there are a handful of numbers you need to know religiously.

There are as follows:

1. Cost per book.
2. Average sale price.
3. Average payout per book.
4. Sell through rate.
5. Cost per lead.

Cost Per Book

This is clearly one of the most important metrics to know as you begin to build or continue to grow your book business, whether it is fulltime or just a side hustle.

A common mistake I see ignorant newbies making, is that they don't accurately assess what the actual cost per book is to them. It's almost as if they are trying to fool themselves that they bought right and everything is fine.

Let me give you an example of what I mean. Let's say that a couple goes out on a Saturday morning book hunting. They hit multiple places all around their city – such as Goodwill and other thrift stores.

After about four hours of sourcing books, they return home and see that they found 50 books. A typical conversation surrounding that would be something like, "Wow honey we did great today! We only spent like $100 and got all these books! They are worth at least $350!"

Is that really all you think they actually spent? Did they really only pay just $2/book? The answer is certainly not. They are missing two very real costs - sales tax & gas costs. Oh, and also their time.

Assuming they were driving in a small size SUV like I do, they spent at least somewhere between $15-$20 on gas driving around half the day. Also, if they paid an average of $2/book that is another $0.16 in sales tax they didn't account for.

I mention all this not to be a penny pincher, but to show how big of a difference this can make. If we go with $20 in gas spent - that means we have to add $0.40/book + $0.16/book from the sales tax, which brings the REAL cost of the books to $2.56 - That's 28% higher cost per book by simply not accounting for costs accurately. That is a HUGE difference!

A typical net profit of a book business can be about 25-30% net if you run an airtight business. You never know how much your profits are being slashed if you aren't tracking this!

Remember - it's all about buying right. You need to find sources where you can get books as cheap as possible.

When you start your business, you need to file a sales tax ID. Once you get this, you can file it with your vendors and cut out the 8% or more sales tax that you typically have to pay on these books. All of a sudden you just reduced your costs by 8%! The best part? A sales tax ID is free. Get one ASAP.

Final thought on this: This process never ends for you. You need to always be evaluating your costs per book every time you venture out.

PRO TIP: Keep a simple written record of your costs with you in a tiny notebook or on your phone while you are out finding books. I use the app "sheets" on my phone

---

Average Sale Price

Average sales price helps you effectively indicate two major things:

1. Are you sourcing the correct kinds of books?
2. Are your books priced correctly?

So, what do I mean by - the correct kinds of books?

There are millions upon millions of books out there. Some are worth pennies (such as mass-market paperback romance novels) and some are worth hundreds (textbooks).

If all you are doing is going out and finding paperbacks with an average sale price of $9, guess what? Your average sale price is going to be about $9!

$9 is extremely low for people going out and cherry-picking. You should be in a much higher range around $15-$20 ASP (average sales price).

Yes, the majority of your books are going to be lower dollar paperback on average, but when you find those textbooks and higher dollar books, they will help bring up your average ASP.

I'm not saying you should leave low priced books on the shelves - I am simply making a point here. You should always grab books where you can make a 2x-3x (or more) on your investment.

PRO TIP: If you are not having luck finding text books at your local Goodwill and thrift stores it's because that particular store pulls them before they put them out on the floor. To find textbooks, go on places like Facebook marketplace and buy from students.

Average Payout Per Book

This is my favorite metric of all. The reason for this is that it paints the most accurate picture if you are buying right and pricing right in addition to your ASP.

Average payout per book is even more in depth than ASP because you can accurately figure out what your average payout from Amazon per book is. ASP alone will not allow you to do that. Every book is a different size and weight, so the fulfillment fees/referral fees always differ.

While I was cherry-picking back in the earlier days more often, my average payout per book hovered around $7.50-$8.00/book, which is a great range to be in (especially since I was getting books for .20 at the time – an unheard-of price).

When I made the jump over to bulk and started shipping pallets instead of individual boxes, my ASP and my average payout per book slid dramatically down to the mid $5 range.

This was due to two things: we were able to collect lower priced books since our shipping per book went from as high as $0.40/book down to $0.11/book.

That meant that these $7-$8 mass market paper backs were pulling down both of those metrics, especially since there are a lot of them!

When you are cherry picking you won't be grabbing these books since the margins are too tight, but when you go bulk you want to monetize everything you can since you have already paid for every book in your possession.

At the time of this writing, I am collecting ANY book that has a profit of at least $1.00 or more (assuming the rank is realistic to eventually sell).

2020 update: Our average payout has risen to about the mid $6.50 range now (driven by better bulk vendors). Also, our volume has gone up.

Sell Through Rate

This can be somewhat of a balancing act for many sellers. The "gold standard," if you will, for your book sell through rate should be around 20-25% per month, or 5-7% per week.

Often times, you can use that metric to easily paint an accurate picture of how your business is behaving.

First of all, if your sell through rate is unusually high (say 30-40%) you can draw a few conclusions from that. First conclusion is that you may be selling your books far too cheap which means you are missing out on profit and eroding your margins.

Second, the average rank of the books you are selling is low, thus they move much faster (not necessarily a bad thing).

However, longer tail books (books that take a little longer to sell) typically make you more money because they are more expensive to the consumer.

All these metrics as a whole will give you a clear cut, bird's eye view on your entire business and ultimately lead to you making the most ideal business moves. I can't tell you how many times I have looked at my data and it has helped me course correct quickly and effectively each time.

Cost Per Lead

At the end of the day, you need book leads coming in day in and day out. Ideally, these leads will be "free", as in you do not have to pay to purchase these books.

However, in order to set up this incoming flow of leads it will cost you in other areas like website creation, hosting, and potentially spending money on ads.

Currently I run two separate sites at the time of this writing, all centered around selling and receiving books.

The two sites are austinbookdonations.com and bookpallets.com. Go ahead and check out either of these if you are interested in modeling them. Feel free to even copy them!

Now, focusing on my incoming book donation funnel - austinbookdonations.com, I know that on average, my cost per lead is roughly $2.00 a lead.

This site isn't that "seasoned," and it can already make me as much as $2,000 a month in sales.

Right now, we typically get a handful of leads or more per week, with over 75% of them working out in terms of a "good pick up".

By a good pick up, I mean it's actually worth our time to drive and pick up a large pile of books. Sometimes we get leads that may have one bag of children's books. That's not going to work.

So, what you want to do is divide your total overhead for your site and any ad costs by the number of actual leads you ended up using.

For example, let's say you don't advertise, but you have a business plan for your website that costs $20/month.

Because you are smart and used SEO for your site name, you still end up getting about 5 leads a week, or 20 per month. Only 75% of these works out to being great leads, so you go ahead and account for 15 leads per month.

20 x .75 = 15 leads

That would come out to $1.33/lead for that month. Based on my numbers and history with pick-ups, you are going to crush it on these in terms of your return on investment (ROI).

Once you get traction, I recommend doing some sort of sponsorship if you can. Make sure to religiously monitor your lead costs. Don't let them get away from you.

PRO-TIP: KNOW YOUR NUMBERS. I can't emphasize this enough. It is of the utmost importance.

Tracking Key Performance Indicators (KPI's)

Aside from knowing your numbers religiously, you also need to first implement, then track benchmarks for you and your team on a weekly basis.

Remember, a ship with no rudder has no way of steering in the direction the captain wants to go.

For most of you, I would be tracking the following KPIs at a minimum (there are several more you can track):

-Number of books listed
-Number of pallets scanned
-Number of cold calls made to new sources

Now, this isn't something that you record at the end of the day and week and look back on just for the fun of it. You make this list first thing Monday morning or Sunday night, in order to set the tone for the week.

These are example goals you have to hit. So set each metric up as its own line item and put down what your goals are for each as follows:

Week of Oct 1-6 KPI's

	Goal/Actual
Pallets scanned	20/18
Books listed	1000/900
Pallets sent out	1/1

What I love most about tracking this, is that it reminds you that the reason you aren't hitting the sales numbers you want, is due to your performance.

If you are constantly missing your numbers, but the numbers you put up are essential to hitting your revenue/profit goal, well guess what? You probably shouldn't be expecting to get to that exact goal.

This allows you to plan accordingly and make adjustments along the way to keep you going in the right direction.

Recently, I upped our targets for our weekly numbers thinking that we could all just work much harder and faster to attain the goals.

What I quickly was reminded of is that we are all humans.

We have limits to what we can do. It wasn't realistic for us to throw up the kind of numbers I desired unless we got more help.

Because I had the numbers that would justify the returns, I immediately went out an hired another employee in order for us to attain the goals. Now we are crushing our numbers!

Guess what? Now it's time to raise our goals again ☺. If you are having trouble determining what your benchmarks should be for certain categories like this, my advice would be to give it time and constantly assess.

First, you need to optimize every single process that goes into encapsulating every one of your steps of production.

Do your scanners have comfortable standing mats? Are the bins positioned close and strategic for quick sorting? Do you have a pallet tipper and sorting table?

Are books pre-graded for your listers for ease and efficiency? Are boxes pre-made for quick packing? Do you know for certain you can get as many pallets this week that are crucial to keep your guys busy?

Once everything is set up nicely and efficient, you want to take note of how long each step in the process is taking everyone. How long does it take to go through all pallet? How many books can your lister or you, list per hour? On average, how many books can you fit into a box for your outgoing pallets?

Once you have weeks of data from these different actions, you can formulate reasonable goals based on historical, REAL data.

This is great because you can now assume with some degree of certainty the goals you write down within your capabilities can be hit consistently.

Armed with that data you can now set a realistic goal of revenue and profits – make sense?

Cash flow vs. Your Burn Rate

Anyone out there can start a business. On the other hand, starting one and continuously growing it cash flow positive is a much different story.

With a business such as selling media online, it can become a tricky balancing act. There are a couple key things you need to focus on in order to become successful at building your business in this industry.

Forecasting and pre-planning is HUGE for this business model. The most important question you need to ask yourself is this - At what point will my cash flow intersect with my cost of goods (your burn rate)?

The reason this is important is due to how much you need to "front load" cash into this business. You need to realize that it could takes several months to hit your stride and get your cash flow to the point where it is covering your expenses.

For most people that try to go straight into bulk books it could equate to you plowing in cash for 5-8 months before you start to see any kind of meaningful return on cash.

Let's start with an example of someone who has 0 books in inventory and is committed to spending $2,000 a month on books on a consistent basis until they hit that equilibrium.

0	500	$1.00
Starting Inventory	Books Listed Per Week	Average Buy Cost
$0.12	5.0%	$12.00
Inbound Shipping Per Book	Turn Rate Per Week	Average Sales Price

(All pictures used in these graphs are provided by @thebookflipper – follow him for awesome data and advice as well)

Based on these above numbers, it's going to take you a minimum of about 16 weeks until your cash flow equals your $2,000 burn rate into books. At that point, you have reached equilibrium and you do not need to worry as much about the money you are plowing into inventory consistently because it will start to fund itself.

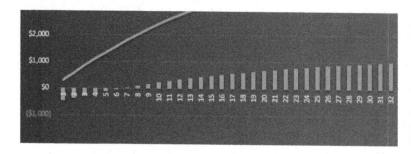

(Bar graphs shown as "weeks". The amount you are getting every week as indicated on the bar graph)

What you need to do is find out how much you want to make in this business (try and be reasonable about what to expect!) then you can work backwards in order to find out what it is going to take to get there.

For many of you, you might realize that this is not realistic for the capital that you have on hand.

For example, if someone wanted to build a $500,000 a year business (in sales – Roughly $100,000 in profit), you would have to spend upwards of $6,000 a month on books alone. At that level you would need a warehouse and you would have plenty of other expenses to go along with it.

For this example, you would have to go 18 weeks just to hit equilibrium in cash flow. But remember, now you have warehouse costs, some labor, trucking, utilities, etc. So, in reality, you would have to go somewhere between 38-45 weeks until your cash flow is covering everything.

All the while, you aren't making a dime. Is it starting to sink in now? This is why I advocate building up your cashflow as cheaply as possible in the beginning. Start in your garage and stay there as long as possible.

In our first example, you can easily work out of your garage and accommodate those numbers – as long as your garage is empty ☺.

You could also get into a storage unit (ideally climate controlled, etc). None of these options is going to be "easy". It can be annoying and uncomfortable, but if you aren't able to handle that then this business model isn't for you.

There are several other ways you can keep your cashflow in check along the way that I personally utilize on a weekly basis. I will share with you my favorite one.

My favorite way to keep my cash-flow in check is by selling wholesale pallets to other sellers that are beginning their journey into bulk. The ideal clients for this are smaller and are still working out of their garage or storage unit.

Since larger vendors won't typically work with a smaller seller such as this (since they won't pick up full semis), these smaller FBA sellers benefit by getting books from you even though the price they pay is higher.

What I typically do is charge double what I paid for my pallets to other sellers. With economies of scale on your side, you can get a discount when buying dozens at a time.

You can also offer personal delivery to that person's residential location for a fee of say $75. This is doing a service to you both, since that buyer would have to rent a truck for much more, and spend hours of their time and energy picking up this load themselves.

It gets even better. If you build up a good relationship and deliver good enough books that they come back for more you can create yet another win/win.

You can drop off new pallets and pick up the old pallets, which gets them out of their way so that they don't have to take them to the dump or find a way to donate them. By the way, that all costs you much more money.

You can then turn around and batch them in with your own duds and sell them to several different buy back companies.

Cha-ching. You make money on the initial sale, the delivery fee, and the dud monetization. All the while, providing a great done-for-you service.

The best place I have found to find other FBA booksellers is on Facebook marketplace. Put out a free ad or two on there and you should get some of your first few bites.

If you like this wholesale route, there is nothing stopping you from making that your full-time business model. There are wholesalers in every single industry. It is a completely viable business model, and one that more individuals should consider.

Ebbs and Flows

This is a continuation of the cash flow segment but deals with more variables.

You need to get good with making cash-flow predictions on a bi-weekly basis so that you can predict what you can and cannot spend on books and other expenses.

This will help you with over-buying or expanding too early, and will give you the confidence you need to make smart busines decisions.

As I went through the early days of my book journey, I did something that I doubt many other sellers did. I kept a numbers spreadsheet (bar graphs) outlining every 2-week payout I was getting on a regular basis.

I also had my inventory levels documented as a bar graph side by side of each other to see any similar relationships.

This allowed me to see my cash flow increasing as my inventory levels increased. What was interesting to me (since I was newer at the time), was that my cashflow never quite seemed completely correlated to the number of books I had on hand in my inventory.

It certainly grew with it, but not in ways I had expected. It was kind of erratic. Textbook season (August/January) had really put some big spikes in my numbers, and summer time threw me off as well.

I remember in July I was sitting there scratching my hand wondering how I had almost doubled my inventory, yet hardly saw any increase in the amount of sales.

Then, the next month it was like a bomb went off. I more than doubled my sales overnight and I was completely ecstatic. My payouts were also MUCH higher than I was used to. I used those payouts to quickly roll more inventory back in to "feed the beast", and was soon disappointed because September and October were not nearly as good as August.

My cash flow also had returned to a more "normal" level. I soon reasoned that I'd better remove both August and January out of my calculations for cash flow if I wanted the most accurate picture of what my cash-flows looked like on a bi-weekly basis. This helped me a ton when making more informed decisions.

When payouts were great from those two months, it was just icing on the cake for me. Funds were put aside for a rainy day.

Once I had a grasp on my cash-flow numbers, THAT is when I took a leap into a small warehouse, because I knew I could afford it with the numbers I was already throwing up. In other words, the cashflow from my business was supporting the new roof over my head.

A common mistake I see newbies making is that they have a big August or January, thinking it is the new norm and they get trigger-happy.

They jump into a warehouse they can't afford or start hiring based off of inaccurate sales numbers.

As sure as the sky is blue, they then have a panic attack a few months later as bills are piling up. They can't seem to understand why they are in the situation they wound up in.

Let's make sure that you don't put yourself in this situation. Take the time and break down the numbers. Set up projections like a smart business person should, and execute on them as best as you can. I believe in you.

PART SEVEN: FINAL THOUGHTS

I honestly can't think of an easier business to start and one that requires such small amounts of capital than a book business on amazon.

It still to blows my mind to this day. For most of you taking the leap and going on to build your own book business empire, you will most likely get bored or want to move onto other things.

That is fine. Just make sure that you build your business to the point where it operates without you at the helm. You see, this type of business is all about producing cash flow.

It's going to be hard to sell this type of business, so you should never bank on building it to sell.

That is, unless you are able to create a business model around selling books outside of amazon where you are able to collect a customer's info.

You have to understand that you don't own any of these customers that you are selling to on third party platforms. Companies such as amazon do.

Big investors throw large multiple out to companies that have their own platforms and customer lists. If you want to build your book business up to sell. You need to remember that as you start.

You'll have to take sales online through your own ecommerce website. You'll need a way to capture customers email addresses and other info. You will have to spend a TON of money on various forms of advertising in order to get your site ranking on places like google.

You see, the problem with selling books is that the average ticket value is very low. If we were to look at mine in particular, we are netting roughly $6.50 per book, after everything.

That means you only have that much money to spend to acquire each customer, which is hardly enough. Goodluck trying to make a profitable sale.

The best you can hope for would be to break even on the sale, get the customers email address, and be able to market to them on the back end for more books in the future.

Selling products at a profit of $6.50, requires you to sell large amounts of books to turn a decent profit, so the sooner you get started creating your own website and fulfillment the better. It's going to be a long road (like anything else worth building) so be prepared for it.

I took another approach with my business. I do want to look to sell this one day, so long as the payout is substantial enough.

Since I am always pondering how to make things work, I knew there had to be another way to take my sales and customers and make them my own.

The one thing I was missing was a higher ticket item that I could use to then invest in advertising, should I choose to. That would allow me to build and scale something exponentially.

That is when I decided to build my company and website around wholesaling.

With a healthy average profit per pallet, I was able to provide myself plenty of wiggle room for investing in advertising/customer acquisition.

If you are curious of ways to invest in advertising your services for this particular business, I would highly recommend that you think outside the box and not just go for traditional paid ads.

Partnerships with influencers in the space is going to be your best bet by far. You want to focus on someone who already has the exact audience or avatar you are looking to target.

I'd recommend cutting in influencers a percentage of each sale they can generate you, or even giving them a small slice of equity once you have a track record.

Also, you want to specifically work on your referral generation for leads.

For my site bookpallets.com, I offer a nice $50 finder's fee for every single lead sent our way that ends up doing business with us. I just received another referral from this last night. I can guarantee you traditional paid ads would have cost me 2x-3x more than that.

Time for A Rant!

As I sat down to write this section of the book on a rainy day, I found myself stopping to take a nice big sip of my steaming hot coffee the morning after Thanksgiving. As I savored that delicious sip, I started to reflect on the past year.

Then it dawned on me - It's incredible how far my wife and I have come and how many changes there have been to our lives in 2020. Boy, I so thankful for everything I have. Just two short years ago, I didn't even know that this media business opportunity existed.

I was a "struggling" entrepreneur that was doing EVERYTHING I could to figure out the next best legitimate thing was and get my life headed in the direction that I wanted.

Everywhere I looked it seemed like everyone was making millions online but me. How were they doing it? Why hadn't I figured it out yet?

As important as all the information in this book is for you, you should know that this section is even MORE important.

I want you guys to know something. MOST of what you see, hear, and daydream about is NOT real when it comes to making money online.

I know I have briefly touched on this prior in my book, but bear with me because I am going to make a point here in a minute.

Online marketers are everywhere. You can't hide from them. There is always going to be the next best thing thrown right in front of your face constantly.

NO, none of you are going to make millions or even thousands working from home in your PJ's. The only one getting away with that are the online marketers themselves. Erase that BS from your head.

The only ones making "millions" are these same marketers promising you can "build a million-dollar business on amazon in 90 days" and spending thousands of dollars a day on Instagram and Facebook, putting themselves in front of anyone dumb enough to think that they could accomplish something like that.

Why is it that these marketing gurus online continue to capitalize on people like you and I? It is simple. Pain. Buying something that will get you out of pain is on everyone's mind, whether it is conscious or subconscious.

In addition to that, people don't want to work hard. They want the magic bullet. They want the secret. They want the "fast track". These guys who put out this content know that.

I have very seldom ever paid for a single course, consulting call, or private backroom access group. I came close to purchasing a $2,000 course, to actually grow an existing business of mine, but I am so glad that I didn't. It turns out the individual teaching it has no real-life experience as a consultant. They just consult others how to be a consultant....huh?????

You need to be careful who you pay, who you listen to for advice, and who you put your trust in. Do your homework first. Now, let's transition back now into my point.

I want to express to you guys that if you are still going through life unhappy with your job, your career, or your 9-5 (whatever you want to call it) I know exactly how you feel.

If you are absolutely DYING inside to work for yourself and become an entrepreneur, I completely sympathize with you.

Here is the good news - If you have this feeling in the first place, you're headed in the right direction – trust me.

Back in the day, I would have given anything to work for myself in a profitable business. It ate at me daily and it completely consumed me. It gave me a drive to devour so much business information and consistently alter my mindset.

However – let me caution you here. If you think that once you get to the "other side" things are going to be easier, you are dead wrong. I know because I am there. I make a full time living working for myself.

Buying and selling different types of media is HARD work. It's not easy money. It can be back breaking (literally).

Since I started doing bulk books, I have worked 60 hours a week or more. We have scanned over 1,000,000 books by hand, listing tens of thousands, and move around 1,000 lb boxes all day.

There are constant problems such as cash flow, suppliers missing a deadline, accounts receivables that are late, trucks breaking down, employees missing work when you need them – you name it. It's all part of being an entrepreneur.

What hit me recently was that I wasn't even ready to be an entrepreneur when I wanted it so badly.

I didn't have the right mindset. I didn't have the patience to get through hard challenges that were out of my control. I didn't know how to manage cash flow, make effective sales calls, build business relationships, or be a LEADER (and I am still learning all these – the process never ends). The list goes on and on.

Would I change a thing? Would I go back to my cushy 9-5 sales job making 6 figures?

NO. Why? Because I LOVE what I do. I was made for hard work. I happen to love books – actually I am obsessed with books. Products sell whether I am working or not.

I am fortunate enough to have a business model that makes money while I sleep and doesn't depend on me to drive 100% of the revenue.

Believe me when I say, I get up every morning amped to go to work. I am always up at the crack of dawn.

Some days I am so consumed that I forget to drink water and eat my lunch. My wife even has to remind me to be home on time consistently and stop me from working on weekends.

Just recently, I took an entire month off of work and went on a road trip back home to California to get away from the Texas heat.

Although the trip was incredible and absolutely needed, the last two weeks I wanted to get back to work. I couldn't wait to get back to put in more work and build up the business further.

The truth is, I love to work - I really do. When I get to put my love for work and energy into building my own empire, that is when the magic really happens.

So, I ask you now – are you willing to do what it takes? Are you mature enough to know what you need to work on within yourself and improve upon (ex: mindset)?

Are you willing to wake up when it's still dark out every day and be the first one to the "office"? Are you ready to have people's livelihoods dependent upon your actions?

I could go on and on with these types of questions for you. If these intimidate you, that's because they should!

Be honest or you will be doing yourself a disservice.

If you are bought into putting in the hard work and you are ready to get on the journey of self-improvement, this business is going to be a great fit for you.

I don't think there is a faster way to start a real, money making business (that involves selling physical products) than this type of business.

Great things are in store for you guys. This book was simply intended to introduce you to this opportunity at hand – if I had to write everything there is to know down in a book and outline every single little thing, it would be a 1,000-page book.

What I have in store for you is better. Head on over and subscribe to my YouTube channel Hayden Aquilon and there you will find every single video you need to make you successful in this business. I outline all aspects of finding, sourcing, listing, and repricing books.

I also want to invite you to join my free Facebook page where you can ask ANY number of questions to our community. It's a massive resource that you need to take advantage of.

You can find it at **_Hayden Aquilon Books_**. I personally spend several hours a week in there and will gladly answer any of your questions!

Now, with that said – It's time for me to wrap this up.

The #1 excuse for most people is that you "don't have time." The specific issue here being, "I want to build my own business, but I don't have any idea where I can find the time to get started. Between work, the kids, and friends there is no time for me to educate myself and source for products."

I get it, it's hard. I have a family too. Our son was literally just born when I started my journey. Not only that, but I was running our small coffee business full time as well.

I would get up at 5am and work until 2pm and then immediately go source until 5 pm or later. My wife and I also opened up the shop on weekends too. 80-hour work weeks were not uncommon. Guess what? My wife isn't a stay at home mother either. She works a high demanding, stressful job.

Do you have any idea how little sleep we've gotten the last year? Any idea how long of work weeks we've put in? In spite of it all, we made it happen. And you can too!

If you are someone reading this that is single with no family, you really have NO excuse. The other day, my friend asked me how my business was going and we got into the details of it all.

He was amazed and said the usual responses such as "wow, congrats I wish I could do that". "Wow you are so lucky that you got to that point of quitting your job".

I love this particular friend to death, and because I do, I had to interject. To me, the simple answer for him was how he could achieve similar results by making changes to his everyday life to start him on the right path. I bet a lot of you reading can identify with this next part.

This guy in particular is working full-time for a corporation in sales. He does pretty well for himself, but he hates the "corporate grind".

Here is what his typical week looks like:

Monday: Dreads going to work like everyone else – I hate Mondays.

Tuesday: Man, I hate Tuesday too....at least it's one day closer to Friday.

Wednesday: Well at least its "hump day" – half way there! I can see a light at the end of the tunnel! Oh, and there is happy hour today, WOOT!

Thursday: Ouch, I am hungover pretty bad, but tomorrow is Friday and I can make it through. Oh, and I get to go out and have drinks with the crew again tonight.

Friday: TGIF!!! ...I'm hungover again, but not as bad as Thursday, I'll be okay. Time for the weekend! Can't wait to go downtown tonight with everyone.

Saturday: Wouldn't you know it? I'm hungover yet again, but hey, YOLO! I can drink this hangover away out on the golf course today. "hair of the dog" right?

Sunday: Wow, I'm wrecked from all the fun I had over the weekend. At least it's Sunday, I can recharge and watch Netflix all day. Almost as soon as you are relieved you get to be lazy all day, you realize that Monday is around the corner.

Then the "Sunday scariez" kick in like they always do, ruining your whole Sunday afternoon and night. One of your final thoughts that same night before bed being, "If only I could figure out a way out of this hell."

.... And <u>THAT</u> is how the vicious cycle goes on, and on, and on, (of course with different obstacles) until you wake up at age 65 wondering what ever happened to making your dreams a reality.

You need to get off that hamster wheel and get serious as soon as possible. You need to be intentional with your time.

If we look back on my friend's week you could easily start planning to take action and get yourself that much closer to a transition into your own business.

Let's look at this with a different mindset now.

Monday: You get off work, go straight to the gym and start your night off energized with a good attitude and feeling of healthiness. You put aside just 30 mins to an hour of time to strategize and come up with a game plan (not finish, just start one!). Then go ahead and unplug and watch Netflix!

Tuesday: You have your game plan in the back of your mind and are excited about it – you think about it during the day and it gets you motivated. You go to the gym again, feeling good and starting from a place of being in the zone. At this point, you've got a rough idea of where you are going to source and you have mapped out the most efficient way to start getting media.

Wednesday: You can't wait for work to end, not because you're going to happy hour, but because you are going to make 3 stops at various sources to get products today!

Equipped with your sources you have mapped out, you jump in your car and spend the next 2 hours finding products.

Once home, you feel excited and accomplished. Wow, you found dozens of good products today and have a potential of $300 sitting in your trunk. What an awesome start.

Thursday: I have an idea. What if I use half of my lunch hour to work out, that way I can go directly out and source after work instead of happy hour again? You decide to do it.

You come back from lunch with a second wind, feeling good instead of coming back after eating a big pile of Chinese food.

You suddenly realize something – you have done pretty well closing deals this week. You wonder why that is.

Then it dawns on you, you now have a REAL _why_ behind your actions. Your subconscious is helping you achieve your goals. If I close more deals, I can make more money and help fund this side hustle to eventually make it full-time!

You again say no to happy hour, as you would rather go out and source product and get you that much closer to building your storefront and making more money (it would also be much better not to be hungover for once at work on a Friday).

Friday: You wake up rested and charged. You head to the office and close some great deals at work. You've done good all week and decide to take it easy tonight – no big deal. All weekend you plan on hitting garage sales and estate sales where the cheap deals are.

Saturday: You wake up early and head out to several garage sales, getting there before others do. You do pretty well for yourself and spend very little.

On one of your last stops you end up making small talk with the garage sale home owner and they end up telling you they have TONS of books in their house they would like to sell as well. SCORE.

Sunday: You spend your morning listening to podcasts and listing all the books you found from the week. Of course, you check your amazon app to see that your sales have doubled recently. The magic is starting to happen!

Do you see how these small daily choices completely change the path you continue on? That is ALL it takes. Tiny choices that you make daily are what determine where you end up. This isn't a secret.

Do you want to know the best part? Once you get going and start engraining these practices, they become a habit. Practicing these new habits daily helps you gain MOMENTUM.

Once you have momentum, things become easier. Not only that, but many more opportunities naturally open up for you.

Playing the Long Game

ANY business you build is going to be a marathon, not a sprint. You can't just be a good business owner one week and decide to let things slip the next.

You need to develop strong habits mixed with will power to keep you going.

If some days you feel like sourcing products and others you don't, you are already on a path to nowhere. If that is your mindset, all this will ever be for you is a hobby.

I see thousands of people like this in my Instagram feed, especially in the same industry.

They put up photos of the $1,000 in sales they did last month and how they are "killing it". This goes on for a while and then they drop off the face of the planet shortly after.

The next month you see they are now part of a multi-level marketing scheme selling health supplements and absolutely "hustling and killing it!"

Several months later, they are now the "king of crypto."

This same thing goes on and on and they continue to spin their wheels, moving on to the next best thing.

There are three good reasons for this that you need to watch out for:

1. They get bored of the same routine and industry. It's lost its excitement. Because of that, they are losing momentum.
2. They hit some sort of small road block they couldn't overcome.
3. There is also something BIGGER and BETTER on the other side of the fence ("better opportunities").

What is amazing to me is how many people get relatively close to "making it" in one venture, but they throw in the towel a little too early because of one of these three things.

I bet you that if they actually knew how close they were, all three of those reasons above would fly right out the window.

They would 100% commit to staying the course, I guarantee it. Do not let this happen to you! **<u>Play the long game!</u>**

I'm wishing all of you the best of luck out there, and I am rooting for every single one of you.
I want to leave you with my favorite quote of all time:

"The harder I work, the luckier I get." — Samuel Goldwyn

Remember that. Cheers to your journey!

Made in the USA
Las Vegas, NV
03 April 2021

20688111R00105